"This is a tremendously smart and highly readable resource full of valuable insight and practical guidance. FEAR-LESS NOW is an excellent articulation of one of my favorite themes, the importance, value and intelligence of being brave enough to relax! How wonderful! Read on and heal! This book provides a deep understanding of the healing power of Yoga and its spiritual foundation. Its aim is to liberate the individual into serenity, love, and the conscious realization of one's unity with Infinity."

Erich Schiffmann
Author of *YOGA: The Spirit and Practice of Moving into Stillness*
www.erichschiffmann.com

"Ingrid Bacci's book *FEAR-LESS NOW* offers a profound understanding of the connection between physical, emotional and mental healing, and helps us to achieve a deeper understanding of our spiritual essence. This book offers a way of achieving a happier serenity, focus and strength we all desire and as a result offers us a possibility of regaining our human dignity and integrity."

Richard Brennan Author of *Change your Posture – Change Your Life*

A Manual for Healing and Self-Empowerment in a World of Crisis

Fear-Less Now

Ingrid Bacci, Ph.D.

BALBOA.
PRESS
A DIVISION OF HAY HOUSE

ISBN: 978-1-4525-5148-7 (sc)
ISBN: 978-1-4525-5160-9 (e)
ISBN: 978-1-4525-5149-4 (hc)
Library of Congress Control Number: 2012907769

Balboa Press books may be ordered through booksellers or by contacting:

Balboa Press
A Division of Hay House
1663 Liberty Drive
Bloomington, IN 47403
www.balboapress.com
1-(877) 407-4847

Because of the dynamic nature of the Internet, any web addresses or links contained in this book may have changed since publication and may no longer be valid. The views expressed in this work are solely those of the author and do not necessarily reflect the views of the publisher, and the publisher hereby disclaims any responsibility for them.

The author of this book does not dispense medical advice or prescribe the use of any technique as a form of treatment for physical, emotional, or medical problems without the advice of a physician, either directly or indirectly. The intent of the author is only to offer information of a general nature to help you in your quest for emotional and spiritual well-being. In the event you use any of the information in this book for yourself, which is your constitutional right, the author and the publisher assume no responsibility for your actions.

"Stepping Out", Provided with permission by Artist, Kevin McCarthy.

Any people depicted in stock imagery provided by Thinkstock are models, and such images are being used for illustrative purposes only. Certain stock imagery © Thinkstock.

Printed in the United States of America
Balboa Press rev. date: 05/23/12

Also by Ingrid Bacci:

The Art of Effortless Living

Effortless Pain Relief

To Vivekananda, with infinite gratitude

CONTENTS

ACKNOWLEDGMENTS

Life has a way of teaching us what we need to learn. Each step in that learning, whether through difficulty or through opportunity, comes as a gift that broadens us and deepens our sense of purpose. I have been given many gifts. Some came in the form of physical illness or emotional pain. Such blessings in disguise have been the fodder that enabled me over time to understand what it means to live well and to offer a helping hand to others.

Many of the gifts I have received have come through good fortune. From my earliest years, I was exposed to some of the great philosophical and religious traditions of the world. While they have all fed me, I am especially grateful to two of the greatest teachers of Eastern traditions, Vivekananda and Yogananda. Each of them combined an extraordinary knowledge of ancient traditions with the capacity to offer concrete and effective guidance in meeting life's challenges with grace and gratitude. These two giants of both heart and mind have been my most important spiritual teachers.

Three practical healing disciplines have helped transform my life from ignorance, confusion and pain, to greater wisdom, peace and strength. They are the Alexander Technique, Craniosacral therapy, and Yoga. Each of these disciplines roots itself in the body. Studying each has helped me to free myself from the physical, emotional and mental chains of my existence.

Many clients have helped me grow, and family and friends have been a constant support. Thank you to my father, for his sensitivity and his refined mind; to my mother for her extraordinary courage; and to my sisters and my brother, for sharing with me life's path. Gratitude to my dear friend and editor Susan Lanzano, for the meticulous and delicate way she has improved my writing.

And thanks to Kevin McCarthy for contributing the image of his sculpture "Stepping Out".

INTRODUCTION
The Journey to You

Truth is one; the sages speak of it by many names.
-Rig Veda

If you're human, what you want in the end is pretty simple. You want to feel dynamic and empowered. You want to feel loving and loved. You want to feel calm, peaceful and contented. Finally, you want to feel that you are making a meaningful contribution. For each of us, these things make up our sense of being truly free and fully ourselves. We all want freedom, and whether consciously or unconsciously, that's what we spend our lives pursuing. Yet few of us achieve it. Few of us find our way to feeling fully empowered, dynamic, valuable, peaceful and happy, being who we need to be, and feeling that who we are is also good for the world. We may try hard enough, but things tend to derail us along the way. And so, despite our very best efforts, we continue to live with those all too familiar daily feelings of entrapment: fear, pain, anxiety, anger, disappointment or purposelessness.

Why is this? Is there a solution to this problem? Do we have to accept that life will never fully give us what we want or that we will never really know what that is? Is there a way to approach life that can give us the freedom, the empowerment, the sense of joy, purpose and fulfillment that we seek? If there is, then what are the reasons that we fail to achieve these goals? What are the tools we need to rely on, and the perception of life we need to cultivate, in order to find what we all desire? The explorations of and answers to these questions form the subject of this book. The pages that follow aim to give you a manual for living peacefully, happily, successfully, meaningfully and freely in the universe.

1

The lessons provided are both old and new, rediscovered in every generation by seekers after the truth, and codified in some of our most venerable traditions.

Those traditions, whether they are spiritual, mythological, philosophical or psychological, tell us that *we are our own worst enemies.* We are the ones who create our own purgatory and our own hell. These same traditions also tell us, that *we are our own angels.* We hold within ourselves the keys to our healing and to experiencing life as an amazingly creative and fulfilling journey. Clearly, then, there is a paradox in the human condition. We are the engines of our own pain and self-destruction, but also potentially the masters of our own liberation. If we can understand how we create pain and suffering, perhaps we can also understand how we can create freedom, and we can step into a world filled with wonder, purpose and peace.

The fact that we are the source both of our suffering and of our freedom has been described in countless ways through the ages. Visionaries, poets, dreamers and philosophers have explored this truth in their own language, spiritual seekers have dived to its depths and climbed to its heights, myth makers have used imagery and stories to tell the tale of transformation from personal suffering to redemption. Such seekers, visionaries, philosophers and myth makers bring us a unique gift: the gift of articulating the ultimate challenge of the human condition. The following two stories each illustrate the nature of this challenge in different ways. The first story involves the West's first official encounter with Eastern spirituality and religion; the second involves the wisdom embedded in the West's celebrated myth of Oedipus.

Paradox Encountered: West Meets East

It was September, 1893. The United States had just finished celebrating the four hundredth anniversary of the discovery of the Americas by Christopher Columbus. As part of this celebration a World Fair held in Chicago had brought together the greatest scientific advancements of the Western world, proclaiming the triumphant achievements of industry. The elite of American and European society were in attendance. As a grand finale to the World Fair, a World Parliament of Religions was opening on that day. Representatives of the world's religions were in attendance to round out the festive event with discussions of humanity's higher spiritual aims. The program of speakers had been prepared months beforehand. Unexpectedly, however, an electrifying individual who had no official place in the Parliament's program took its audience by storm. His name was Vivekananda.

A thirty-year-old impoverished mendicant monk from India, with no credentials other than his many years of spiritual practice, and no entry ticket to the Parliament, Vivekananda had slept in an abandoned railway car a few nights earlier. Despite his disheveled appearance and obvious poverty, the power of his larger-than-life personality had attracted the attention of important individuals who obtained permission for him to participate in the Parliament. Although Vivekananda was the last speaker of the opening day of the Parliament, by the next day he was the gathering's star attraction.

The first embodiment of the ancient wisdom of the East ever to visit the industrialized West, Vivekananda magnetized the audience with his message. For years after the Parliament was over, he also acted as a personal teacher to some of the most distinguished members of American and European society. People flocked to his side to hear him speak, and not only because his interpretation of spirituality seemed compelling. A living expression of his own message, he was irresistibly attractive. Princely in appearance despite his rags, he exuded the authority of wisdom and the tenderness of love. His bearing struck home. Despite all their material comforts and achievements, people had a deep hunger for something richer than what they already knew, and there was something about Vivekananda that satisfied that hunger.

Vivekananda's message was clear and to the point: First and foremost, he told his listeners, you have the capacity to fully experience your own freedom. Your life need not be limited to a controlled pursuit of accumulation and survival; instead it can become a glorious adventure of the spirit in its complete unfolding. Second, beneath their differences, for all great spiritual and religious traditions the pursuit of freedom is the universal goal. In their purest form, these traditions aim to offer the individual *a clear road to his or her own full freedom.* You know you have found that road when you experience peace, joy, power, meaningfulness and flow in the current of life. Third, the freedom we all seek is an internal experience, not an external achievement. Freedom is in its essence a way of feeling, living in and relating to life. This internal freedom is distinct from and independent of external status or achievement, and is a necessary foundation for any lasting happiness. While inner freedom can and often does generate a harvest of external rewards, such rewards are not so much goals in themselves as they are the natural outgrowth and result of attaining inner freedom.

Vivekananda's audiences ached to hear his words. They were affluent, but they were not necessarily happy. Something had gone wrong along the way. Their focus on external achievement had not given them the inner sense of satisfaction that they longed for.

Vivekananda warned that the West's materialistic culture held a dark danger. When people do not pay attention to nurturing their internal state, when they focus too much on external goals and material possessions, they activate psychologically self-destructive drives rooted in and fed by fear, competition, insecurity and greed. These drives can eventually annihilate their own material creations.

Vivekananda visited the West at the height of its materialistic optimism and achievement. It was expanding in every direction with opportunity and growth. Yet the monk prophesied correctly that the culture, driven as it was by competition and greed, would self-destruct. Twenty years after his predictions, Europe exploded into World War I. Another twenty-five years later, the entire planet was engulfed in World War II. Today, global crises continue to reveal the ongoing costs of living in a culture that glorifies consumption at the cost of sacrificing the most meaningful search of a person's life: the personal quest for self-awareness, authenticity, peace and love.

Vivekananda's warning is even more relevant today than it was over a century ago. Global warming, increasing natural disasters, life-threatening levels of pollution, crippling poverty, famine and disease, insufficient health care, limited educational and employment opportunities, extreme concentration of wealth in the hands of the few, endemic corruption, exploitation, widespread violence, wars and terrorism, and planetary financial collapse: these are all examples of large scale events and situations that in one way or another result from destructive individual human motivations run amok. Such events also reach deep into every individual's life, causing anything from stress or disappointment to loss, disease, suffering, and perhaps even death. No one is immune. Where you do not feel the results of such events directly, in the loss of a home, loved one, health, career or nest egg, you nonetheless may feel them not only through daily tension and anxiety, but also through an insidious growth of cynicism and despair. Life can seem exploitative rather than liberating, and your relations with others controlled by fear, greed and manipulation rather than by creative vision, honesty, generosity and collaboration. Yet it is just when things get truly unpleasant that people begin to have the motivation both to seek for better solutions and to work steadily and patiently on implementing them. The time for that is now.

A society is the outgrowth of the interactions of its members. The macrocosm reflects the microcosm. Each of us as microcosm plays our part, through our thoughts, feelings and behavior, in creating the macrocosm we live in, a macrocosm that is now so profoundly off center that even planetary survival seems threatened. Each of us needs to liberate ourselves from the tentacles of that macrocosm, creating our own healing and wellbeing in the face of the odds. Each of us also, by changing ourselves, can help change the world. Because we create the world, the world can change if we do. We can opt out of the dynamic of fear, pain, competition and anger that fuels our lifestyle. We can take healing ourselves seriously. Along the way, we can free ourselves from being society's slaves: we can work from pride rather than from fear; we can manifest what is really meaningful to us; and we can own the incredible gratitude of a life well lived.

Vivekananda became a spiritual celebrity in the West, awakening people to the recognition that despite their affluence, they had bargained for way too little in life. He taught them how to aspire to more. We all need to ask ourselves whether we, too, do not want more. Not more things, but more contentment, more inner acceptance and love, more peace, more creative vision and more strength.

How much better could life be? Most people are so used to feeling bad and so unaware of the real alternatives open to them that they either no longer experience their distress consciously or, if they do, they think it is unavoidable. Vivekananda showed people that negative states of mind and feelings of suffering are not unavoidable. They are bad habits. In fact, negative feelings and states of mind are actually signals to each of us, asking us to wake up, take action, and transform our lives.

Here are some of the signs of pain that could be telling you your own life is off track: feelings of restlessness, a need to be on the move, obsessive thinking, chronic feelings of anxiety, anger, depression or disappointment, criticism or self-criticism, feelings of inferiority or superiority, envy of others or the drive to prove yourself to others, frustration, low energy, exhaustion, chronic illness. If you recognize any of these in yourself, your spirit is crying out to you for change.

Every negative feeling or self-destructive state of mind has its corollary in self-destructive behavior. Here are some of the external behaviors that correspond to the inner dis-eases of the spirit that plague virtually all of us: constant activity and "to do" lists; restlessness and continually being on the move; achievement, achievement and more achievement; consumption, whether of sex, food, alcohol, clothes or other products as a primary source of gratification; and focusing on meeting others' needs or needing to have others meet yours. These all signify inner dis-ease. If you suffer from any of these pathologies—and who amongst us doesn't—you have lost your way. Losing your way doesn't make you either unusual or bad. It makes you human. Welcome to that strange thing, the human experience. It's full of illusion, full of errors and mistakes, and full of opportunities for learning, self-correction and meaningful self-transformation.

Alienation, anxiety and dissatisfaction have been part of the human experience from time immemorial because we keep on losing sight of the fact that true freedom is internal, and that it is only by gaining internal freedom that we can create a self-sustaining universe around us. As a species we look in the wrong place for our sense of identity and validation. *We look outside ourselves to soothe an internal ache instead of cultivating a healing relationship to our insides.* That mistake sets in motion the miseries of life, along with the exploitation, neediness and greed that result from these.

Vivekananda taught his listeners that there is *a practical, step-by-step process for finding the state of being that makes us truly free on the inside,* and consequently also optimally powerful and constructive on the outside. In this teaching, he was in accordance with the great traditions of the East that do not distinguish between spirituality and psychology. These spiritual systems are sophisticated approaches to the psychology of mind, body and spirit that show you how to systematically apply a few simple principles to freeing yourself from suffering. If you learn and practice these simple principles, you can find your way to serenity, joy, dynamism and personal power. You can then use those internal states to achieve something meaningful and useful in the world, rather than sacrificing your sense of wellbeing to endless fears and needs based on the insecurity that drives people to consume, own, achieve and compete. The forthcoming chapters describe in contemporary terms the practical processes that give us freedom.

Paradox Unveiled: The Oedipus Myth

Vivekananda taught that owning personal power is about *unlearning* psychological and physical habits that make us self-destructive and end up being destructive to others. Some spiritual traditions speak of this process of unlearning as a journey from darkness to light. Others use terms like ignorance, false consciousness or sin to describe how it is that human beings manage to forget themselves and set about creating a personal hell that is then mirrored in a social hell. Philosophy, myths and poetry also tell this story. For example, the Greek philosopher Plato described the human condition as follows: We are like a society of people living in a cave, with our backs to the opening. The Sun, the source of all reality, shines through the cave and projects shadows onto the wall. Human beings, however, mistake the shadows for reality and live turned away from the Sun, which is their true source. To find our freedom and happiness, we have to reverse our own tendency to look away from our source, and stop relying on illusory types of happiness that end up defeating us. We have to release our ignorance of who we are, the ignorance that creates our tendencies toward self-sabotage.

In Western mythology and literature, no figure represents this truth more powerfully than Oedipus, the tragic hero of Sophocles' play *Oedipus Rex*. Oedipus was the son of King Laius and Queen Jocasta of Thebes. Before he was born, his parents consulted a blind man named Tiresias who was the oracle at Delphi. Tiresias prophesied that Oedipus would kill his father and marry his mother. Horrified, King Laius and Queen Jocasta decided to do their best to avoid this fate. They gave their infant son to a herdsman with orders to kill him. The herdsman instead took pity on the boy and gave him to another herdsman. This man gave the infant Oedipus to King Polybus and Queen Merope of Corinth. Being childless, that king and queen adopted Oedipus.

Oedipus grew up thinking he was the biological offspring of his adoptive parents. This single fact, that he did not know his origin, led to tragic mistakes. With the best of intentions, he made a mess of his life and damaged those he meant to care for.

Growing up as the young crown prince of Corinth, Oedipus heard rumors that Polybus was not his father. He refused to believe this and consulted an oracle for confirmation. The oracle, however, did not answer his question directly, telling him instead that he was destined to kill his father and marry his mother. Horrified, Oedipus decided to leave the king and queen whom he thought were his real parents. He departed from Corinth, and eventually found himself on the road to Thebes. On that road, he met, quarreled with and killed a man he did not know. That man was his real father, King Laius of Thebes.

When Oedipus arrived in Thebes, he successfully solved the riddle of the Sphinx, a terrible creature who blocked all passersby from entry to the city, devouring them if they could not answer her riddle. Later, Oedipus married King Laius's widow, Queen Jocasta, and thereby became King. Unbeknownst to himself, he had married his mother.

Oedipus had several children by Jocasta, time passed and life was good. Eventually, however, things started to turn sour. When a plague devastated Thebes, Oedipus consulted an oracle. The oracle told him that the plague would only be lifted once the murderer of the former king of Thebes had been punished. Oedipus swore to find the murderer and punish him. Alas, he eventually discovered to his horror that he was himself King Laius' murderer, that Laius was his father, and that his wife Jocasta was his mother. Queen Jocasta committed suicide when she heard the news. As for Oedipus, he blinded himself in self-punishment, piercing his eyes with a brooch belonging to his wife and mother, and then exiling himself from Thebes.

Oedipus was a tragic hero. The enduring resonance of the Oedipus myth derives from the fact that it reminds us symbolically that like him, we are the tragic heroes of our own personal dramas. Oedipus meant well, but because he did not understand who he was, he called down on himself and others a terrible chain of events. In our own lives, *our intentions are good, but we unintentionally contribute to our own and others' suffering* because we don't come from a solid foundation of self-knowledge.

We make bad choices for the wrong reasons. How and why we do this is the subject of the next few chapters.

Like Oedipus, it may take us a long time to recognize that we have created a large part of the mess we are in. That doesn't mean we are bad, but it does mean it's time to reconsider what we view as important and what motivations we follow in life.

Thinking he was someone other than who he really was, Oedipus projected his false beliefs onto the world. This inevitably led him into destructive and self-destructive behavior. Like Oedipus, we are plagued by *false beliefs* about what will actually give us happiness. These beliefs *encourage us to live a life that fails to bring us the level of contentment we seek* and that ends up bringing us disappointment, frustration and pain instead.

Despite his misperceptions, Oedipus was convinced that he was doing the right thing for himself and for others, and he enjoyed a measure of success in his life. We, too, during the course of our lives are sometimes certain that we are going in the right direction, and we may even enjoy external rewards that strengthen us temporarily in this conviction.

The truth eventually caught up with Oedipus, when he realized that his actions had generated the devastating fate he wished to avoid. Like Oedipus, at a certain point most of us realize that the way we have been pursuing life does not help us reach a goal that will truly satisfy us, and that we may well be doing the opposite. At this point of recognizing the truth about how we have been living—an experience that can happen multiple times in a lifetime—we typically feel tremendous pain. Even though we may not, like Oedipus, lose our material possessions and external stature, we nonetheless recognize that the person we have been and the things we have relied on for our sense of self-worth can no longer sustain us. This painful situation is also the point at which transformation begins.

Oedipus became a wanderer on the face of the earth. The time of being without a home was also the time of self-discovery in which he came to terms with himself. Like Oedipus, once we recognize that our lifestyle has not given us what we truly need, we become metaphorical wanderers on the face of the earth. The old rules no longer apply, and we go through a process of discovery and creation that, pursued with passion and depth, gives us a far richer sense of meaning.

Oedipus' life process dissolved a false ego structure and replaced it with wisdom. If we can better understand our own psychological and spiritual dynamics, we can free ourselves from the painful ego structures that make our lives less than ideal. This is our true journey, a journey celebrated by every great spiritual, religious, philosophical and mythological tradition.

My Own Journey

As the Oedipus myth implies, life is a journey of self-discovery. As a child, my own quest for self-discovery first showed itself in the intense curiosity I had for the big questions. "Who am I?" "What is Truth?" "How do I know others exist?" By the time I was a teenager, I had begun to read philosophers like Bertrand Russell and Alan Watts. As an undergraduate at Harvard University, I studied philosophy. After completing a fellowship abroad at Cambridge University in England, I continued these studies in the United States, earning a Ph.D. in philosophy from Columbia University in New York City. I especially loved philosophers who studied the nature of consciousness—the existentialists and phenomenologists, with their quest for understanding the perennial challenges of the human spirit. When I eventually became a professor of philosophy, I most enjoyed teaching the work of the Danish religious existentialist Soren Kierkegaard, a deep thinker who spent his life passionately searching for and writing about purity of heart.

I now know that my intellectual pursuits were interesting, but they were just baby steps into the waters of life. They may have been important for my evolution, but they did not touch my being beyond the level of cerebral curiosity. Life, however, has a way of compelling us into deeper waters. It was not long before what started as an intellectual interest in understanding what living was about became a driving practical need for physical and emotional healing. In my early thirties I suffered a complete and unexpected physical breakdown that lasted for several years. I was crippled, debilitated by both pain and weakness. The best of medical care, including numerous drugs and several hospitalizations, failed to help me move past the connective tissue disease that doctors told me might be incurable.

This was a very dark time in my life. It was only after numerous attempts at conventional healing, followed by many months of depression and hopelessness, that I began to take my first tentative steps in new directions that proved to be healing. Inspired by reading about unusual people who had healed themselves of intractable diseases, I began to observe myself: my body, my breathing patterns, my tensions, my thoughts and my emotions. I began, with help from a few gifted healers, to find threads of connection between all of these aspects of myself and the very real physical pain and disability that were crippling me. Over the years that followed, I plunged into an intensive study of the mind-body connection and of numerous forms of bodywork. On a spiritual level, I explored writings in Buddhism, Chinese philosophy, Hindu philosophy and esoteric Christianity. I investigated my own dynamics both psychologically, somatically and spiritually. I studied energy and high sense perception to gain a deeper appreciation of the underlying realities that govern our functioning. Through diligent practice of meditation and related training, I also developed psychic skills. The conjunction of all these processes gradually led to a complete physical healing. They also gave birth to my second career as a somatically based healer, medical psychic, author and teacher of self-transformation.

In the course of my personal journey, I came to recognize that mind, body and spirit are not only connected; they interpenetrate and influence one another in ways far beyond what we imagine. This truth is eminently available to anyone who cares to explore their somatic processes deeply. Those who doubt the complete interdependence of mind, body and spirit do so because they live life divorced from the rich inner experience of the unconscious that lives in their own bodies.

My early life was blessed with all the things we generally want in life: well-intentioned and caring parents, an excellent education, travel to many countries and abundant opportunities for self-enrichment and professional recognition. Yet it has been the years of trial, of poor health, divorce, financial stress, and of gradually building a creative integrity-based career that have given me the greatest blessings I have owned: the opportunity to heal from my own unconscious pain and to find a joyful foundation for my life that offers me the tools both for physical, mental, emotional and spiritual self-empowerment and for helping others on their path.

My first two books, *The Art of Effortless Living* and *Effortless Pain Relief,* articulate some of my insights on the interconnections of mind, body and spirit, as do the audio programs I created to accompany them. My practice over the last twenty years, as both a craniosacral therapist and an Alexander Technique teacher, have offered me the blessing of working closely with thousands of clients on their own healing, and of learning from them. So too have the self-healing retreats I have taught throughout the United States and Europe.

This book, *Fear-less Now,* represents for me the culmination of my learning to date. In the chapters that follow I offer you the path to your freedom and full self-empowerment as my life and studies have led me to understand that path. It is a path that is both highly practical and personally mystical. It is also unique to you as an individual. In defining that path, I have drawn from personal experience, from the healing experiences of numerous clients, and from the wisdom of great psychological, philosophical, religious and spiritual traditions of the world. It is up to you to make that path one that works for you.

In the pages that follow, you will find numerous recommendations and exercises to help you on your way. Many of these can also be accessed in audio or DVD format through my website (www.ingridbacci.com). The tools I describe are meant not only as tips for the moment but also as suggestions for lifelong practice. Each tool is something that can be put into immediate use for practical benefit today, tomorrow, next month and next year.

Before turning to the practical steps that can heal us, however, we need to be clearer on who the enemy is that lives inside us. What keeps us addicted to disempowerment? What makes us unable to access a sense of life as being fully meaningful and liberating, even perfect? It is inside us that we must search for the answers to these questions. Because we are all controlled by our own inner darkness, by forces that drive us without our understanding, we need to see these forces for what they truly are. We also need to find the determination required to eradicate them. *Part I* of this book, therefore, explores what it is inside each of us that keeps us disempowered. This exploration creates a foundation for the work of self-transformation. *Part II* takes you as the reader through a step-by-step process of self-healing and transformation, a process that will enable you to own your full potential and to fully realize the gifts you can bring to the world around you.

PART I
The Problem

1

The Knot of Fear

You can never control the effects of fear yourself, because you made fear, and you believe in what you made.
-A Course in Miracles

In ancient Asia Minor, in the part of Macedonia that was at that time called Phrygia, an oracle consulted by local priests predicted that warring between rival factions would come to an end when a man with a wagon entered the town. That man turned out to be a poor peasant named Gordius, who was soon seen driving his ox-cart into the marketplace. The priests declared Gordius king and rival factions accepted his rule. Years later, Gordius' son Midas succeeded his father as king. He dedicated his father's ox-cart to the gods, tying it with a large knot to a post in the town center. The knot was an intricate and complex Turkish one that had no ends exposed. Over time, the ox-cart and its knot became a shrine, and an oracle foretold that whoever was able to untie the Gordian knot would become lord of all of Asia. Many attempted to loosen the knot, but none were able to do so until Alexander, later known as Alexander the Great, wintered in the town of Gordium in 333 B.C.E. When he could find no end to the knot, Alexander took his sword and sliced it in half with a single stroke. He solved the problem of the Gordian knot by taking an unorthodox approach. The prophecy associated with the knot was also fulfilled, and Alexander went on to become the ruler of all Asia.

Gordian knots are intractable challenges whose solution requires taking a radically original approach. What, then, is the Gordian knot of our lives? If we are capable of liberation and fulfillment, what is it that actually ties us down? It might seem that for each person the answer to this question is different. One person might think that the primary problem he needs to solve is his lack of a loving partner. Another might feel that if only her health would improve, all would be well. Yet another might feel that his real problem is lack of money. Yet achieving any of these won't necessarily make you free or happy. You can be married to someone you consider your ideal mate, have excellent health and financial abundance, and still be miserable, restless or anxious. The real problem lies deeper.

As Vivekananda reminds us, it is an internal attitude we bring to life that generates all the other problems from which we suffer. *The critical issue facing each of us is not what we have or don't have. It is how we feel inside:* sad or happy, anxious or contented, irritated or peaceful. The fundamental knot of our lives lies in our emotions. The solution to our problems lies in developing internal mastery of our emotional life. If we can feel peaceful, alive and joyful deep inside, we can swim through life's problems with a sense of grace. Then we can also use our inner strength to achieve blessings such as health, abundance and satisfying relationships. But if we make our emotional state dependent on what we have or don't have, achieve or don't achieve, we can't be happy. We will suffer from fear, desire, restlessness, anger, impatience, jealousy, depression, disappointment, any and all of the host of negative emotions that can toxify our lives.

The Gordian knot we must cut through is the discontent we experience as a result of harboring negative emotions. As different as all of these emotions seem to be, *they all have a single root.* Anxiety, restlessness, worry, impatience, frustration, greed, jealousy, resentment, anger, and other negative emotions are all rooted in *fear.* It is fear that creates greed, anger, jealousy, worry, disappointment, irritation, impatience, and anxiety. It is fear that keeps us from owning our happiness. So long as fear holds a place in our hearts, we cannot be free.

How can we free ourselves from fear? Is it possible to do this? Let's begin to answer this question by taking a closer look at the dynamics of fear.

The Self-Destructive Face of Fear

None of us want to feel fear. We'd love to be free of it. Ironically, however, we cherish it. How? When we are afraid we tend to think that the problem we have is not the fear we feel but whatever it is that we are afraid of. We tell ourselves that if the situation or event that we fear would go away, we would no longer be afraid. We think that the problem is not in us. Instead, it is in the situation, event or person that we perceive as causing our fear. Yet in taking this attitude we actually rationalize fear. We justify it. We give ourselves *reasons* for holding on to it by telling ourselves that the cause of fear is outside, not inside.

Many of us spend an enormous amount of time making room for fear. We are afraid that we will get up too late; afraid that we will miss the commuter train; afraid that we will do poorly in school or at work; afraid that the car will break down; afraid that the weather will be lousy; afraid that our children will disappoint us; afraid that someone won't like us; afraid that we will get sick from the food we eat; afraid that we won't get hired; afraid that we will get fired. In each case, *we give ourselves reasons to justify the way we feel.* We assume it is reasonable or appropriate to feel the way we do. By giving ourselves reasons for our fears we give fear life. Once we give it life, we live as its victims.

You can be afraid of your boss, a colleague, your parents, your big brother or sister. You can be afraid of disapproval from your friends or of abandonment by your loved ones. You can be afraid that someone won't like you and you can be afraid that someone will try to cling to you or make excessive demands. You can be afraid of failing your exams or of failing in your profession. You can be afraid of succeeding. You can be afraid of people of a different religion, race, social group or nationality. You can be afraid for your health or for your family's health. You can be afraid of terrorism and you can be afraid of war. You can be afraid of financial loss or deprivation. You can be afraid of losing a job, of not getting a job or of not rising fast enough in your job. You can also feel a nameless generalized anxiety every day, an anxiety many of us attribute to the stress, pressures and demands of everyday life. And of course, you can be afraid of dying.

When we feel fear, we may say to ourselves that we are right to feel it. After all, this is a dangerous world, and we would be fools, misguided, or living in make-believe if we weren't afraid. We may tell ourselves that we have good grounds to fear our boss or our parents, because they hold power over us, because they have bad tempers, or because they disapprove of us. If we fear for our financial security, this may seem reasonable enough if we have lost a great deal of money, have lost our job, are concerned about future employment or are retired and don't know if we have enough to live on. If we fear for our health, we may justify this on the grounds that we have had hard times with our health in the past; or that toxic effects of environmental poisons are everywhere, or that cancer is all pervasive. It may seem eminently reasonable to be afraid of terrorism or war because people die every day due to terrorist attacks and we have either been in wars, lost family or friends to war, or make a habit of watching news about war on the television and internet. As for dying, why not be afraid of that? After all, it's the end of life as we know it. All these fears may sound rational enough. Yet they are not. Fear may be natural, but it's not rational. Why?

The challenges we face during our lives are sometimes enormous. They can and sometimes do include financial distress, controlling bosses, negative colleagues and friends, judgmental associates, discrimination, health problems ranging from the annoying to the life threatening, abandonment, loss and deprivation, floods, earthquakes, war and death. Life is a hard playing field. It is not meant for sissies. Let's not confuse the issue of whether or not fear is justified with the issue of whether or not life is tough. Life *is* tough.

No one wins at life in the sense of getting a ride free of major shake-ups. Though some have it easier than others, everyone gets their share of bumps. In this sense, and in this sense alone, fear makes sense. Fear is an expectable and very human reaction to difficult, sometimes seemingly unbearably difficult, situations. The issue, however, is not whether life does or does not have challenges, and it is not whether we do or do not on occasion feel anxiety. The issue is *what you want to do about that fact.*

Do your fears contribute to or impoverish your life? Does fear cripple you or strengthen you? Is it possible that your fears *multiply* life's challenges and provide a *greater share of pain and misery* than you might otherwise have? If this is the case, doesn't it make sense to begin systematically slicing through the Gordian knot of fear? Doesn't it make sense to practice challenging fear and gradually releasing yourself from its grip? Anyone who wants to improve the quality and authenticity of life must do this. You cannot find your full self if you cannot challenge your fear.

Fear is always fear *of* something, and that something always seems negative. Yet fear of negative occurrences does not help us either to control them or to make them go away. Fear worsens many challenges, invites numerous additional problems into being, and poisons our quality of life.

The social and political exploitation of fear has always been a dominant force in the control of one person by another, one group by another, and one nation by another. If someone holds the ability to put you in fear, they can control you. Those in power know that exploiting fear is to their advantage. Fear was the engine that brought Nazi Germany to power. It continues to be a major tool employed by governments around the globe. Fear of reprisal and fear of loss hold most people in work situations that bring them stress, insufficient pay, and too little control over their own lives. Fear gives pharmaceutical companies power and takes away human faith in the body's capacity to heal itself by natural means. Fear drives the wars that spread across the globe. And fear is a major force in a consumption-based commercial system, where the addiction to consumption is driven by the need to fit in, to be better than, and to have more.

While it's easy to recognize the repressive and oppressive social uses of fear, its oppressive role in our own emotional dynamics is harder to discern, because when we feel fear, we tend to tell ourselves that our fear is reasonable. Only once we see the complete irrationality and destructive impact of fear in our own lives can we begin to let go of justifying it and focus our primary attention on doing everything we can to release ourselves from its satanic grip. The next explorations make this increasingly clear.

Fear Destroys the Present

Each moment that you feel fear contributes to worsening your life. The clearer you become about this fact, the more likely you are to begin healing from fear. When you feel fear you feel bad. What's more, that bad feeling in the pit of your stomach, or the feeling that causes you to sweat or that makes you racy is a feeling that exists in the *present* moment. The present is *all you have!* Every time you feel fear, you are feeling terrible right now, and right now is all there is.

Life is nothing but a sequence of present moments: one *Now*, followed by another *Now*, and then again followed by another *Now*. In your lived experience, there is neither past nor future. The past is gone and the future is not yet here. The only thing you can manage is *Now*. When you feel fear, you defile *Now*. You do that by focusing your attention on a *future* anticipated negative event or situation. Whenever you feel fear in the *Now*, you desecrate, demolish and destroy your *present* in the name of a *non-existent future* that currently exists *only in your mind*.

The real problem is not the possible future event that we worry about, although we may say to ourselves that that's what it is: that the problem is what will happen tomorrow at our job, or how our sweetheart is going to treat us this evening, or whether the stock market is going up or down in the morning. The real problem is the present moment that we destroy in the name of our concern about a future event.

When we fear something, we project from a *certainty,* which is our present experience, to an *uncertainty,* which is an unknown future. We take a non-existent negative future event, bring it back into our present as if it were real, and feel terrible. We find a reason to be anxious in this *Now,* and then in the next *Now* and then again in the next *Now.* All in the name of something that does not yet exist, and may never exist!

Uncertainty in the face of the unknown is the ultimate source of fear. But if what will be is an unknown, is there any reason to paint it in dark colors? Life itself is an unknown. Can we embrace it? If we cannot, we relate to all of life like some of us related to our first dive off a diving board: with fear and trembling. We can stand there quaking on the diving board of life, or we can trust and dive in. Those are the choices. They happen every single moment, every single nanosecond, of our lives.

Work with the exercise below to clarify for yourself how much you may justify feeling fear in the present on the basis of something that has not yet happened and may not happen. This will support you in the process of learning how to release fear.

Exercise: Do you justify fear?

1. Write down everything you can think of that you are afraid of, no matter how trivial. Include things you are afraid of doing; things you are afraid might happen; reactions you are afraid others might have to you; fears about your health, your looks, your relationships; fears about the environment, the society, politics, finances, death.
2. Now write down the reasons you give yourself for being afraid about each thing you have listed. List as many reasons as you can think of.
3. Ask yourself these questions as you look at the reasons you give yourself for feeling afraid. When you feel

afraid, does your reason involve something that is happening right now, or that you anticipate but has not yet happened? Are you acting and feeling as though something that has not yet happened will happen? Can you become more aware that the real problem is not the future that you are afraid of but the present that feels unpleasant when you are afraid about the possibility of a future event that does not yet exist?

4. Notice what your body feels like when you are afraid. Does your stomach or neck grip? Do you sweat or get butterflies? What do you say to yourself when you feel afraid? What kind of images come to mind? Clarify for yourself the exact sensations and images you have when you are in fear, and recognize how unpleasant they are.

5. If your fear involves unpleasant impressions that you justify by reference to a future that hasn't happened, can you let go of it? Can you recognize that it doesn't serve you to feel fear? Be patient and systematic with this process, and it will gradually yield results.

Fear is a Habit

Fear is not only an ingenious device for feeling bad in the present moment. It is also a habit that breeds more of itself. The more frequently we feel fear in the present, the more likely we are to feel fear in the future. Let's say you have a friend who is very critical of you, and you are afraid of confronting that person. If you are afraid today, and don't resolve your fear and address the issue, you will also be afraid the next time that this person criticizes you. Each time we give in to a fear, it solidifies its hold over us and becomes stronger.

Many people wake up each morning with low-grade anxiety and restlessness. From the moment of opening their eyes, their minds occupy them with the pressure of things to do, commentaries on what has been or will be, and various other concerns. This internal pressure cooker doesn't stop. It doesn't leave them alone. The pressure cooker reflects the impact of habits of mind built up over years of facing each day as a series of demands on their time. The sense so many people have that life controls them and that they cannot take charge of their lives guarantees living in fear.

Each moment of our lives we cultivate either habits of fear or habits of freedom from fear. The *present moment is our moment of power.* It seeds our future. Karma tells us that in the future we reap what we sow in the present. What does this mean? Some people think that earning good karma means performing good actions and earning bad karma means engaging in bad actions. But what is good and what is bad? Good and bad actions are all relative to specific situations. In the end, good actions and good karma are whatever fosters internal peace and happiness, both of which also tend to make us more able and willing to nurture the peace and contentment of others. Bad actions and bad karma are whatever fosters the opposite. Working in each moment to build inner contentment and fear-lessness is the core process by which we build good karma. The more we cultivate positive states of mind now, the more likely we are to experience them in the future. Allowing yourself to dwell in unpleasant emotional states now creates bad karma for the future because it increases the likelihood of unpleasant emotional states in the future, not to mention lowered energy, a depressed immune system and disease. A fear-filled existence is the essence of bad karma. It is a painful existence bedeviled by suffering.

When you feel fear, do not think about how to protect yourself from the object of your fear. That motivation will only sink you deeper into a mud hole. Instead, focus on resolving how you feel in the moment. If you can become more peaceful in the moment, you will not only feel better; you will also address any situation you are dealing with more effectively.

The work of life is the work of confronting fear each moment that it appears. When we focus our attention not on the future but on the present, and work to improve the quality of our present moment, we begin to create a life that we master rather than a life that masters us. Integrating the three exercises below into a daily routine strengthens this process of mastery.

Exercise: Detach from the habit of fear

1. Notice how many of the fears you listed in the last exercise happen on a regular basis. Just as smoking one cigarette leads to smoking the next, so too, feeling nervous or anxious can lead to feeling nervous or anxious again. Think about whether you want to change this unpleasant habit instead of letting it rule you.

2. Practice letting go of fear by shifting the way you feel. To develop the capacity to shift your internal state, you may want to use the MP3 entitled *Empowering Your Intention*, available through my website, www. ingridbacci.com. You may also wish to access a complete set of exercises for creating an internal state of release and peace available through my CD/MP3 series entitled *Effortless Practice*, sold through my website. Alternatively, develop your capacity to shift your internal state by following the instructions below:

   a)   Take ten or fifteen minutes each day to create a warm, calm and soothing environment for yourself. If you like, you can put on peaceful music. Make sure no one will disturb you. Close your eyes, breathe quietly, and let yourself drift for a moment or two. Once you are relaxed, imagine an event or situation that you associate with feeling peaceful, happy and positive: being with good friends, lying on the beach in a gorgeous environment, being hugged by a loving relative, etc. Fully absorb the positive sensations involved. You are moving from a less positive to a more positive state. Once you have done this a number of times, you will be able to shift into a positive state quickly and at will.

b)　　After practicing the exercise in a) above, explore shifting your state *at the actual time that you are attacked by fear.* This is not easy to do initially, but regular practice strengthens your ability.

3. <u>Reframe what you are afraid of in a positive light.</u> If you are afraid for your health, vividly imagine feeling, acting and looking radiantly healthy; if you are afraid of rejection by someone, vividly imagine having a great time with that person and being confident in their presence; if you are afraid of not performing up to capacity, see yourself being relaxed and confident at your job. Reframing is like rehearsing for a play. You program your brain to anticipate and create positive instead of negative outcomes.

Fear Creates What You Fear

Fear *attracts* what we fear. Fear creates bad karma not only in our inner life—in the form of negative emotions—but also in our outer life—in the form of negative events. Negative emotions attract negative events. Oedipus was afraid of killing his father and marrying his mother, and so he did. His fear brought him what he was afraid of. We unconsciously attract what we fear.

The fact that we attract what we focus on is popularly known as the Law of Attraction. The Law of Attraction is a law about our inner state, in particular *our inner emotional state* and its relation to *outer* events. When we focus on something, it is the *feeling* we have around that thought, and not the *content* of the thought, that determines the outcome. Focusing on what you want with a positive feeling will tend to draw positive things toward you. Focusing on what you want with a negative feeling will tend to alienate you from what you want. Let's say you think to yourself that you want financial abundance or a great relationship, but you are anxious or doubtful about your ability to obtain these. Your negative emotion will push away from you the things you claim you want. You will get not the abundance or great relationship that you desire, but the *lack* of these, since your emotional state is one of lack. Fear creates lack, which, in turn, creates more fear. If you want to attract something toward you, you have to focus your attention on experiencing the feeling of joy, power or love that in your mind corresponds to having it.

I had the opportunity to witness the Law of Attraction at work in a passionate relationship between two lovers. The relationship fell apart as a result of the dynamic of fear. The man in this duo was the opposite of a warrior. He was a worrier. He worried that his sweetheart would leave him. Because of this, he called her at all hours of the day and night to gain her reassurance. This man was also consumed by second-guessing and ambivalence. One minute he desperately needed to talk to his girl; the next minute he wondered whether she was right for him. The fear that she might leave him and the fear that she might not be right for him were opposite sides of the same coin in his life. Sometimes he would cling to his lady friend with infinite words of love, or shower her with gifts; at other times he would disappear or avoid her. Eventually, exhausted by all the coming and going, the woman broke off the relationship. The man felt devastated, abandoned and betrayed. He could not see how his own fears had attracted what he feared.

My father was an internationally acclaimed mathematician. He was also an obsessive worrier. More than anything, he worried about his health. When I was a child, his worry habit created what was for me a painful distance in our relationship. After my parents divorced, I would visit my father every other weekend. He would greet me complaining that he wasn't feeling well. His eyes were frequently glazed over with his obsession over his health. He couldn't detach from his fear long enough to connect to his children, let alone experience more pleasure in his life. He missed so much of what could have been his.

My father lived a long but worried life. It was only in his last months, when he realized that there was nothing left to fear because he was dying, that he came to peace. In those months, his spirit became a bright flame. You couldn't look into his eyes without recognizing that he was on a beautiful inner journey. I am sad for him that he was unable to start that journey earlier, rather than at the age of eighty-two, and then only as a result of prolonged emotional, and eventually, physical suffering.

As a practitioner of complementary medicine, I frequently work with the emotional and spiritual as well as physical dimensions of ill health. I occasionally see clients who have driven themselves sick with worry about their health. The link between fear and poor health is neither complicated nor esoteric. Fear exhausts our adrenal glands, contracts our muscles, weakens our digestive function and depletes our immune systems. It creates a greater susceptibility to disease. Fear about anything will contribute to impoverished health. Fear specifically about our body's health aggravates this process. If, whenever we feel symptoms, we worry about those symptoms, we only contribute to further physical stress, which creates more tension and exhaustion, worsens symptoms, and invites disease. We lose sight of the enormous power of our emotions for good or for ill. We see our health problems as the consequence of everything *except* our attitude—genes, the environment, infection from contact with other people, and so on. Our profit-driven medical system invites this self-victimization by encouraging us to see the likely causes and remedies of our dis-eases as out of our control. This feeds the purses of the medical industry, which reaps profit from our fears. When it comes to our health, as well as the rest of our life, wouldn't it be better for us to use the Law of Attraction to our benefit?

Exercise: Make use of the Law of Attraction

1. Make a list of things that you wanted in the past but didn't get: for example, a relationship with a particular sweetheart or new friend, a job, victory in a competition, a raise, financial abundance or an improvement in your health. Looking back, can you see any way in which your attitudes and behavior might have influenced the negative outcome? Were you in any way afraid that you might not get what you wanted? Did this influence how you felt and behaved? If so, can you see how your feelings and behavior might have contributed to your failure to get what you wanted?

2. Make a list of things that you currently want in your life: for example, improved finances, better health, a raise, financial security, a better relationship with your spouse, partner, a family member, etc. Notice if you harbor any fear over achieving these things. If you want love, are you afraid that you might not get it? If you want health, are you afraid for your health? If you want financial security, are you afraid that you might not obtain it?

3. Choose one of the things in your list that you want but are afraid you might not achieve. Imagine changing your attitude so that you see and feel the way you would see, feel and think if you already had this thing. What does it feel like to have what you want? Can you see how your fear drives what you want away, and imagining that you already have what you want makes you not only more peaceful but possibly also more receptive to good things coming into your life? An exercise like this needs to become a daily habit. Practice staying in this altered state so as to gradually and surely improve your ability to let go of fear and attract what you want into your life.

Fear Breeds a Host of Other Negative Emotions

Once we harbor fear, we immediately become prey to worry, impatience, frustration, hurt and disappointment, jealousy, resentment and anger. Our negative emotions are so many variations on the theme of feeling *controlled* by something or someone outside ourselves. Feeling controlled is about fear, for fear has its origins in the sense that something or someone outside us rules us. That something can be our body or it can be another person. It can be a neighbor or it can be a nation. It can be the traffic or it can be the weather. So long as we feel controlled on the inside by something that we perceive as beyond our direct will, we cannot feel safe. If we can free ourselves from this sense of insecurity, we can ride even the worst of life's storms from a strong, centered sense of presence.

Let's say you feel jealous of the attention a spouse or friend is giving someone else. You worry about where this person's interest is wandering. You worry that he or she doesn't care enough for you. You worry that this person will leave you. All this makes you insecure and afraid. You are making your own sense of value dependent on how that person behaves toward you. You are in fear. Your sense of being lovable hangs on the loyalty and love given to you by your friend or mate. You have given away your power. If, however, you are secure within yourself, then you need not have any negative emotions over your loved one's giving other people attention, and you need not try to control their behavior. Even if someone you care for treats you dishonestly or poorly, this does not call for fear, but rather for reevaluating the importance the relationship has in your life. Why would you accept into your life anyone who does not treat you with respect and honor? Ultimately, the only answer can be fear.

Other people's behavior toward you never defines whether you are lovable or worthwhile. How can it? If a passerby on the street spits on you or calls you names, does that make you a bad person? You understand that the person's behavior is his problem, and not a reflection on you. So how can your spouse or a family member or colleague talking to someone else or even cheating on you in some way make you less worthy? It cannot. Similarly, how can someone else behaving toward you the way you want them to behave make you more worthy? It cannot. You are worthy because you are, whether or not others treat you as you would like them to do. The more you own this truth, and neither feel controlled by nor need to control others, the more you win the world's respect.

No one can control your spirit when you own it. Viktor Frankl was an eminent Jewish psychotherapist and concentration camp survivor. His book *Man's Search for Meaning* was listed in 1991 in *The New York Times* as one of the ten most influential books in the United States. It provides eloquent testimony to the truth that we can be the masters of our spirits. Frankl survived four years incarcerated in Nazi concentration camp and lost all his family except one sister to death in the camps. In addition to managing his own tremendous suffering and losses, Frankl was also a profound source of support for numerous concentration camp inmates and survivors, helping them maintain their sense of dignity in terrifyingly brutal circumstances. He realized during his incarceration that nothing, not even the most frightening conditions and terrible suffering, could destroy one's freedom of choice over one's psychological attitude. We are always free to choose an inner state of dignity and self-love.

Exercise: Reduce negative emotions by taking back your power

Make a list of the persons to whom you give away your power and the situations in which you do this. You will recognize this is the case if you tend to feel disappointed, hurt, angry or afraid in a given situation or as a result of someone else's behavior. How are you giving someone or something power over your state of mind? How are you giving them responsibility for how you feel on the inside? Can you take back your right to manage how you feel on the inside? While you may not be able to control others' behavior, you can

31

control how much they affect you negatively. Practice letting go of disappointment, hurt, feelings of betrayal, anger and any other negative emotions toward others, so as to own your own natural dignity and take back control over your internal state.

Anger Is the Other Face of Fear

Does even the emotion of anger have its root in fear? Let's begin by distinguishing between anger as a passing and sometimes strategically necessary assertion of boundaries, and anger as a tendency of personality or chronic habit. If someone keeps on stepping on your foot and doesn't pay attention when you ask him politely to stop doing so, you may need to raise your voice to make the point. That's one form of anger. It's like a thunderclap. It comes quickly, asserts itself, accomplishes its goal, and leaves no residue. Animals use this form of self-assertion every day. Cats and dogs know how to hiss and growl to maintain their space. We need to be able to do the same when life calls for it. If we have forgotten how to do this, or never learned, this is partly a result of the fact that we spent a long childhood dependent on others. If not outgrown, enforced childhood dependency breeds adult habits of submission.

The assertion of anger that quickly passes is a constructive life strategy. Anger can be constructive if it leads directly to action in the outer world to correct a perceived problem without damaging others. Anger at ourselves can also be constructive if it generates remorse that transforms us at a deep level. When anger has a proactive result, it functions as a positive temporary emotion that mobilizes change. This type of anger has no relationship, however, to the *angry reactivity that comes from a sense of disempowerment.*

Reactive anger is everywhere. You see it in the unending irritability, impatience and frustration that are daily fare in a speed-oriented, hectic society. You see it in the voices of criticism, fear-mongering and posturing that fill the political arena. You see fear-based anger in such widely different behaviors as compulsive tail-gating on the highway, bullying at work and in the home and the subtle control dynamics of Type A personality competitiveness. You see it in the underlying hostility that is part of working in an environment where you either try to manipulate people into doing what you want—buying your product, doing the work you assign, or approving of the work you perform—or feel manipulated by others doing the same to you. Reactive anger fuels the constant voice of criticism that so many of us hear in our heads, whether that voice is directed against ourselves—"You did it again, you idiot;" "You're such a failure;" against others— "I would never wear those kinds of clothes, they're so garish and low class;" "Complain, complain, complain, that's all he does;" or against more general conditions—"People are so corrupt;" "You can't trust anyone;" "Politicians are just liars and cheats."

Legend tells us that the Buddha once remarked that anger is a hot coal you pick up to throw at someone else. That coal burns *your* hands! When you feel reactive anger, it permeates your body, mind and emotions, causing intense tension. You reject things as they are. You assume that things being as they are is the fault of somebody or something. You become an apostle of blame. It's "their" fault that things are so bad, and you are angry at "them" and upset that "they" have created this mess. Alternatively, if you think it is your own fault that things are the way they are, you direct anger and blame at yourself, subjecting yourself to a barrage of criticism for your numerous faults and failings.

Anger, bitterness and blame can settle into lifestyle choices, soiling a person's inner state from moment to moment and limiting productive outcomes. Chronically angry people make themselves miserable. They tend to make others miserable as well.

Sometimes the connection between anger and fear is not immediately evident. Take the case of being frustrated and impatient about meeting a deadline. We are angry at ourselves or perhaps at someone else on whom we depend to do their part so that we can meet that deadline. This irritation actually results from fear. It expresses a sense of disempowerment, of something outside us controlling us. Our anger does not really have to do with whether or not we will meet the deadline, although we may tell ourselves it does. It has to do with the fact that we have given control over our internal sense of wellbeing—something that is each person's natural birthright—to someone or something else, and so we need things to be other than they are in order to feel okay. Perhaps we have identified our value as a person with how well we perform. If we don't perform up to standard (a standard usually established not by ourselves but by someone else), we see ourselves as failures. Our anger is then a reaction to a fear of failure, and fear of failure can only arise when we have to prove ourselves by some standard that we have internalized and imposed upon ourselves.

It is not easy to learn how to be more centered in a work environment where demands are intense. Being balanced even in the face of severe stresses and dysfunctional behavior on the part of others is an art that takes consistent practice over months, years and even lifetimes. Most of us need to practice balance, among other things because we long ago gave others power over us. In addition, personal balance becomes important when the people we deal with exhibit control dynamics that have nothing to do with us but rather with their own inner feelings of insecurity. Without a strong sense of balance, we tend to get drawn into the fray, contributing to needless tension and disagreement.

Exercise: Identify the underlying causes of any tendency toward anger

1. Identify one or more situations where you feel angry at someone. How might fear be an underlying motivation for the way you feel? Are you afraid of how others will react if you speak your mind? Do you feel dependent on someone else for your sense of security? Do you feel controlled by others, or by a situation? What would be involved in letting go of giving someone or something else power over how you feel inside? How

would that affect your anger? How might you address
the person or situation differently?

2. <u>Do you know anyone who has a tendency toward
anger?</u> What fear might underlie their anger? Are they
afraid of being controlled by others? Are they reacting
to a fear of not being good enough? Are they afraid
of not being heard? If you can see the fear hiding
behind the anger in others, does this change the way
you might deal with them or how you might respond
to their anger?

Fear Creates Desire and Diminishes the Spirit

Paradoxical as it may sound, if we have fear, we also have
desire. If I am afraid of being abandoned by someone, I desire
to have that person in my life. If I am afraid for my health, I
desire good health. If I am afraid of financial loss, I desire to be
financially secure. Fear creates desire. Desire in turn creates fear,
since wherever there is a desire, there will also be the fear of that
desire not being fulfilled. Buddhism and Vedanta both tell us
that suffering comes from unsatisfied desire, and that unsatisfied
desire is a manifestation of fear. "All misery comes from fear,
from unsatisfied desire."[1]

Desire is different from attraction. Attraction describes the
natural gravitational pull of like to like. While that pull can be
strong, it lacks any sense of craving or need. We can be attracted
to something or someone while also feeling complete within
ourselves. Desire, however, expresses a feeling of incompleteness,
of needing something more than what we already are or have in
order to feel complete and satisfied.

Like fear, desire takes us out of the present, putting us in a
race with time. Desire projects us toward a future state of being or
having that is not currently ours, making us restless in the present

---

1   Vivekananda, "Raja Yoga" (*Vivekananda: The Yogas and Other
Works,* ed. Swami Nikhilananda, Ramakrishna-Vivekananda Center, New York:
1953) p. 582.

and fearful of not achieving what we want. Like fear, desire puts us on a treadmill of constantly pursuing some goals and seeking to avoid others. Freedom, however, is something that has to be experienced in the present, and if we are constantly chasing after what we think we want, we will never feel free.

If fear is the ultimate source of both negative emotions and desire, what is its origin? *Psychologically*, fear starts with being dependent as an infant. Because we are dependent on others for our wellbeing during our early years, we learn to identify who we are with how others see us, what they require or need from us, and the beliefs they have. This influences how we interpret reality, how much we like or dislike ourselves, what professions we choose, what kinds of people we associate with, what models of intimacy we adopt, and what we desire..

Spiritually, fear originates in the sense of *separation* that is a natural accompaniment to the experience of having a body. That experience fosters the possibility of alienation. If we did not experience having a body as separating us from what is outside our body, we would not feel at risk from the outside. Yet because we experience ourselves as separate from others, the possibility of loss or pain arises. Similarly, because we think of ourselves as separate from the rest of reality, the fear of death arises. Death can only be fearful if we identify who we are with our body and therefore with the sense of separateness. Yet separateness is an illusion, because the body itself is a passing manifestation of the universal energy field of which we are all integral parts.

To let go of fear at its roots would be to let go of the sense of separation. Yet the mind says "Of course I am separate. After all, I have a body, I am this body. Therefore I am right to feel fear." This is a compelling perception, but like so many perceptions in life, it is an incorrect one.

Healing from fear is both a psychological process of releasing ourselves from dependency and a spiritual process of releasing ourselves from our bodily identification with mortality and its sense of separateness. *A Course in Miracles* describes the sense of separateness as the origin of our ego, which in turn is identical with the part of our personality that is founded in and reacts to fear. As soon as we identify with the ego, with the illusion of separation from our source, we have to live in fear. Fear, ego, and identification with our body are coextensive. To free ourselves from our ego is to free ourselves from fear. This may be an extremely challenging process, but when it is accomplished, it yields infinite rewards.

The Fearless Self

If we can let go of fear we will automatically let go of all the negative emotions and behaviors associated with it, along with the persistent sense of powerlessness that results from identifying with the body's mortality. Is this possible? Can we heal the psychological dependencies that create the foundation of our personalities? Can we heal from the fear associated with our body identification, our sense of separateness and mortality? I can say the answer is "Yes," but that statement by itself is not helpful, because each of us discovers the truth only through personal experience. You will find out for yourself, through your own journey, how to live in the light of your eternity.

Nonetheless, at this point there is an immediate, realistic and practical answer to the question as to whether you personally can let go of fear. You have to start at the *beginning*. Since fear creates all your ills, if you are going to try to heal your ills, *you have to fall in love with challenging fear and then see where that leads you.* You know for a fact that nothing less than this will help you find your own sense of freedom in this life. This fact should make the pursuit of fearlessness a primary passion.

Every one of us faces the radical life challenge of walking the path toward letting go of fear. It's no wonder that great spiritual teachers tell us we must be willing to own enormous courage to find the road home to ourselves. In the words of Vivekananda,

The greatest error is to think that you are weak, that you are a sinner, a miserable creature, and that you

37

have no power and cannot do this or that. Every time you think in that way, you rivet, as it were, one more link in the chain that binds you down; you add one more layer of hypnotism upon your soul."[2]

If we want to have the best life we can have, we have no choice. We have to challenge and seek to conquer our fear. We have to own our courage. The word courage has the same etymological root as the French word *coeur* meaning "heart." To conquer fear is to live one hundred percent from an open and strong heart. The great spiritual teachers tell us that in the process of owning our courage, our heart-fullness, we can end up in a place where we are truly free of fear. They also claim that we discover along the way that everything we are afraid of actually dissolves in the face of a growing, deep sense of being connected to and part of an eternal universe. That's up to each of us to experience, and we can only experience it by going on the journey.

Spiritual traditions tell us that we are something infinite and eternal beyond our bodies, beyond its experience of finitude and separation. Spiritual self-realization happens, and fear dissolves, when we experience the fact that we are not separate, that we are integrally connected to an eternal and infinite creation. Spiritual traditions also find logical, rational validation in modern science. Scientific investigation confirms that the perception of separation is actually an illusion. Beneath all atoms and particles, all the separations of the visible and tangible universe, lies an undivided and infinite whole. We are each emanations of that undivided and infinite whole, wrinkles in the fabric of infinity.

Fear is an expression of ignorance of the nature of our true being. If you are like most humans, then fear is what ultimately controls your everyday behavior. Yet fear is based on the illusion of separation, and the separation you perceive does not actually exist. Intellectually, most people can, of course, grasp this idea, but the challenge is to grasp it as a practical reality. That requires taking the plunge and working to eradicate fear from your life step

---

2   Vivekananda, "Jnana Yoga" (*op.cit.*) p. 340.

by step, patiently, slowly, methodically, but without swerving from your goal. While this journey takes courage and endurance, once you understand that it is truly your path, life begins to unfold in rather amazing ways, and everything that happens to you, both the good and the bad, starts to have a meaning full of blessings.

Summary

Finding our true selves and living from our core peels away all the superficialities of our lives. The first step in this process is identifying where fear conceals itself within us and how it manifests in our lives. Then we can start to let go of justifying it. This chapter has aimed to make that process concrete and clear. The second step in self-transformation is to examine the self-defeating, self-sabotaging mechanisms that we humans get addicted to in our obsessive search to avoid fear, a search that motivates us to pursue ways of building a sense of security that end up being both ineffective and illusory.

Most people tie their sense of security and self-validation to the pursuit of external goals. Yet this pursuit can never be successful. Not only must it fail. In addition, it actually aggravates the basic problem of fear. Just as alcohol or drugs can give you a temporary high while masking underlying pain, in the same way, the pursuit of external goals gives temporary rewards in a sense of security and power, but ends up intensifying the basic problem of fear. The dynamics of that process form the subject of the next chapter, a subject which, once grasped, allows us to move more easily into the quest for true freedom.

2

Life on Crutches

You will not break loose until you realize that you yourself forge the chains that bind you.
-Gary Renard, *The Disappearance of the Universe*

Most of us quiet our fear by pursuing outer sources of validation and security: money, fame, prestige, and so on. Yet no outer possession and no outer achievement can provide ultimate security. You might get temporary feelings of happiness, power or love from attaining these, but in the end, relying on something outside you feeds the insecurity that makes you need outer validation to begin with.

Your only reliable source of personal power is within. Everything external offers at best a band-aid over an existential wound that each of us is meant to address during the course of our own life in order to transform that life into a truly worthwhile experience. When you seek security from a source of validation outside yourself, you trap yourself into an endless quest that, instead of easing your anxieties, ends up increasing them. By leaning on the crutches provided by these external symbols, you never discover how strong your own legs are.

There are three principal crutches that people lean on to bolster their sense of self-worth: 1) money and financial or material abundance; 2) professional and social achievement; and 3) conforming to social norms. These crutches are infinitely seductive. We finally free ourselves from them when we see that

40

relying on them makes us not more secure, but less so. Let's look at why each crutch, despite its appeal, must ultimately fail us.

Crutch # 1: Money and Financial Prestige

Money by itself is neither good nor bad. It is a tool, useful as a means to an end. Everyone needs some. We need a roof over our heads, and we need to be able to feed ourselves and our families. We need these as a foundation for pursuing higher aims and making a contribution. Financial abundance can also be an appropriate *consequence* of pursuing professional and creative commitments that express our life passions. If you pursue financial abundance as your *primary* goal, however, rather than earning it as a consequence of pursuits you really love, you walk down a path that can undermine your integrity, self-respect, and sense of vision. When you succumb to the temptation of making money for money's sake, and your life focuses more around making money than around creating something you value or offering genuine service to others, the consequences slowly erode your sense of self worth.

Contemporary culture encourages us to equate personal worth with financial wealth. This breeds the temptation to prostitute ourselves for the sake of financial gain. Years ago, I knew a woman who was very well paid as a focus group consultant for credit card companies. They hired her to interview small groups of people with the goal of evaluating what advertising gimmicks might entice people to use their credit cards more. Credit card companies profit from people running up credit card debt. The companies that hired this woman wanted her to help them write advertisements that looked like they were offering an unbeatable deal when they weren't. They were professional rogues, out to fleece their customers with well-disguised, appealing lies.

The consultant helped her corporate clients figure out how to write the most profitable lies. She was embarrassed about this, but not so embarrassed as to consider changing clients and giving up her lucrative contracts. She had an affluent lifestyle. Her children went to the best schools, had piano and clarinet lessons, and enjoyed beautiful vacations in Europe. As for her, she was personable and friendly, but I suspect she masked feelings of discomfort by focusing on the praise she got for her work and by overeating. She traded self-respect for affluence.

All of us sometimes have to take jobs we don't love so as to pay the mortgage and get by until a better time. But when the lure of affluence is there, and for this reason we take employment where we don't really believe in the services offered or the products developed, we run the danger of compromising our sense of self and consciously or unconsciously becoming less than genuinely happy. This consultant said she wanted to leave the work she had, but she never did. She was tied down by her negative karma, her self-destructive mental and emotional habits. Perhaps childhood insecurities had led her to focus on getting approval from others, and this had eventually morphed into an adult habit, but the adult habit only fed her insecurity. She could not trust that she could do socially meaningful work and live a decent life. It was easier for her to perform brilliantly and be handsomely rewarded for meeting the manipulative needs of her clients. Although she was gifted, she did not try to define goals she could be proud of, or work toward making these her source of financial abundance. Instead, she sold herself short and accepted golden handcuffs. Her insecurity controlled her, and insecurity comes down to fear.

It is not productive to point a finger of blame at someone when insecurity controls their actions. After all, we can all recognize these patterns in our own lives, if not right now, then sometime in the past, and possibly sometime in the future. What *is* important is to recognize how self-defeating it is to be controlled by our fears. We can only summon up the courage to challenge them when we see how self-destructive they really are. The consultant's deeper fears made her unable to break her pattern of self-prostitution. In the process, while she no doubt contributed to the manipulation of others, the person who suffered most directly from her behavior was herself. Even though she made money, she lost the sense of pride that could have been hers if she had set her sights higher, and she ended up supporting a system she did not believe in. You can't feel good about yourself if you don't believe in what you do.

We lose our innate sense of decency and humanity when we go in pursuit of money. We get tempted to look the other way if our financial gain causes someone else pain or loss. The more intense a person's need for self-aggrandizement, the more heedless they become of the damage they cause others. Hedge fund scam artists surely don't take tours through the homes and lives of the people they rob, to witness the consequences of their greed. Their own self-involvement is too great to allow them to contemplate these things. They have no inner reservoir of dignity and integrity.

You can reap financial abundance by following your inner guidance, but you cannot find that inner guidance by giving priority to the lure of money. If you succumb to that temptation, you may get money, but you will also get a competitive, anxious or greedy spirit, restlessness and craving, frustration, and a superficial sense of life's meaning. You may also find yourself medicating your inner unease, distress and pain by resorting to food, alcohol, drugs or other types of addictive behavior.

Facing my own cultural addiction to financial security put me through a difficult struggle that took years to resolve. In my early thirties I was married to a man who was a millionaire many times over, and who stood in line to inherit many more millions. Had I stayed married, I would have guaranteed my financial comfort for the rest of my life. My husband, however, was a narcissist and an alcoholic. At the time that I began to become aware of his psychological and physical addictions, I was bedridden with a chronic connective tissue disease, and it was very tempting to stay married. After all, I did care for my husband, I felt very poorly most of the time, and I had no clear medical prospects of recuperation. Living with my husband, I had all the physical comforts of life at my disposal to keep me comfortable for as long as I wanted.

It took me several years to accept the fact that life with this rich but alcoholic man was unbearable, that I was sacrificing myself if I stayed, and that I had to get divorced. I left our home when I was still very sick. As a result of a spiritual mentor's advice, I also accepted a minimal financial settlement from my husband that left me facing financial hardship. Yet once I finally took the plunge and left our marriage, I felt an unaccountable sense of relief. I realized dimly that I had taken the first giant step in letting go of a pattern of dependency that had caused me to let myself be seduced by the charms of an easy life and to overlook the problems of a relationship with a charismatic but angry, controlling, and sometimes violent man. As I look back at that period of illness and crisis, I see that my spirit created a situation that forced me either to sink or to swim. I had either to address my insecurity by stepping out into the world on my own despite chronic health problems and lack of financial support, or to retreat into the golden chains of outer comforts at the cost of my own integrity. I discovered that life crises are often opportunities for growth and liberation.

Living with my husband, I had suffered a form of the spiritual malaise that the existentialist philosopher Soren Kierkegaard aptly called a "sickness unto death." Nonetheless, not a single doctor among the many specialists I saw during my illness raised the possibility that my illness, real as it was on a physical level, also reflected a sickness of the soul. Doctors gave me complicated diagnoses and an abundance of pharmacological recommendations, none of which had any lasting effects and many of which fostered lethargy, confusion and a deadened sense of self.

My growth in self-empowerment, reflected in my eventually letting go of outer comfort for the sake of greater personal integrity, was a key element in my physical healing. It also played a role in my developing a career in alternative healing that focused on the intimate link between mind, body and spirit. In the past twenty-five years, I have worked with countless people whose physical pain and illness were direct expressions of psychological and spiritual conflicts in which they subjugated their own faith in themselves to the seductions of external benefit.

Despite the suffering, illness and confusion I experienced during my period of illness, I view myself as blessed for having stumbled my way into realizing that sacrificing personal integrity for the sake of financial security carries a heavy cost. I was also extremely lucky to have strong moral support from a few key people whom I deeply respected and who helped me on my path in the many moments when I faltered. Others are not always as fortunate as I was. I watched a dear friend lose her life as a result of the conflict she felt between the needs of inner growth and the lure of material ease.

Nan was married to a wealthy lawyer. She lived in a mansion on a large estate in one of New York City's elegant suburbs. She and her husband sported several homes in various parts of the country, all of which Nan devoted herself to decorating with impeccable taste. A former successful entrepreneur, in the years that I knew her Nan spent most of her time occupied with the duties of wife, mother to her teenage daughter and college-age son, and entertainer extraordinaire. She loved mingling with celebrities of all kinds. Despite her affluent lifestyle, however, she was in a very real sense financially dependent. Her husband controlled the purse strings and all their investments were held in his name.

Nan and I met at a lecture that I was giving at a holistic center. We felt an immediate liking for each other and we gradually became close. During this time I began to see that Nan's husband treated her less as a wife than as an expensive maid, and that he was often lavish in his attentions to other women. Nan herself described him as a "predator," yet whenever I asked her if this disturbed her, she would laugh or say her relationship with her husband was excellent.

If Nan had been able to admit to herself that her husband's behavior toward her was degrading, she would have had to take action. This would have destabilized her lifestyle and affected her relationship with her children. Most of us prefer not to see painful truths until we are forced to. It is no surprise that Nan lived in denial of the level of her husband's disrespect and disloyalty. Her conscious mind rejected what she subconsciously knew.

Nan became ill with cancer. Shortly after she told me about her cancer, I had two dreams about her husband. In each dream he was being sexually promiscuous with another woman. I asked Nan if she had considered that her husband might be having an affair. She rejected this possibility outright. Yet the trail of evidence was incontrovertible, and Nan began to work through her own denial. A few weeks later, she confronted her husband over the affair he was having with her best friend. She also broke off her friendship with that woman. Finally, she took steps toward ensuring that some of the family's finances were transferred into an account in her name. When she did this, she told me that she was concerned that if she died, the children she had borne her husband might be left with nothing if he took up with another woman. She wanted to protect her children. Nan also began to consider divorce.

Nan's actions required determination and perseverance, and she was up to the challenge. She had to hold her own against her husband's belittling behavior and her so-called best friend's lies and hypocrisies. She had to own her personal truth, along with the painful recognition that two of the people she cared for most had betrayed her with each other. She had to insist on having a separate bank account, and insist until she got it. As she took more of her life direction into her own hands, Nan's cancer also went into remission.

Unfortunately, after the initial crises had been addressed, Nan's strength of will began to waver. The benefits of the lifestyle she had—its glamour, travel, entertaining—tempted her once again to put aside the more painful reality that living with her husband in fancy environs was also living with disloyalty, control and abuse. Even though her children were now in college, she was no doubt apprehensive that separating from her husband would harm her relationship with them. She decided not to get a divorce and she returned to apologizing for her husband's harsh behavior. Nan's cancer returned.

Perhaps Nan delayed further confrontation with her husband, thinking to wait until her health improved. Yet there was a tragedy in her choice. When we give someone or something else greater importance than our own self-respect, we compromise the deepest part of ourselves. The results can be devastating. Our integrity is the source of our vitality and energy. We can't turn off the valve to our own energy circuits without suffering the consequences. Nan lived one more year before her now aggressive cancer claimed her life. A few months after her death, her husband moved in with another woman. He was remarried within six months. He also quickly sold the home Nan had spent her last year decorating for him. Events speak for themselves.

Our personal integrity is the only thing we can really own. Integrity doesn't require that we deny ourselves the benefits of financial wellbeing. It does, however, require that we not sacrifice our sense of self-respect and autonomy for the sake of those benefits. The problem with making material comfort and its prestige symbols more important than our self-respect is that once the focus on money becomes the primary driving force behind our decisions, while we may feel good about what we *have*, we don't feel good about who we *are*.

Many people fail to take seriously asking themselves how they want to manifest their spirit during their lifetime. Instead, they ask themselves what they want to do to make money. Those two questions are very different. Which question you focus on dramatically affects the course of your journey. When you focus primarily on being financially comfortable, you risk sacrificing strength for security. When you sacrifice strength for security, you make bedfellows with anxiety, fear, anger, and dependency, all of which undermine the quality of your life.

Finding your way to uniting personal integrity with abundance is not an overnight job. It is a slow, step-by-step process with numerous challenges along the way. Some of those challenges are small; others are enormous. Yet if you focus on following this process, it will gradually crystallize into building the right life for you, a life of which you can be genuinely proud. Along the way, you have to let go of the myth that tells you that only after you become financially abundant can you think of who you really want to be. Because we live in a materialistic culture, most of us have on some level accepted living under the influence of this myth.

The exercises below aim to trigger a greater awareness of where each of us is or is not compromising ourselves for the sake of money. If you feel that you want to have money yet not be controlled by your fears around it, these exercises can help you get clearer on how to pursue that goal. Remember that it is the *incremental* daily changes we make that will open up that goal. These exercises are all about small yet consistent changes. Let them serve you on your path.

Exercises: Confronting the financial dragon

1. How much is your self-worth tied to money? Do you feel superior or inferior to others depending on how much money or how many possessions you have relative to them? Do you suffer a loss of self-esteem when you have less money? Do you feel any sense of competition to keep up with others in your neighborhood or social group, when it comes to owning houses, cars, pools, taking vacations, giving your children fancy presents, etc.? Make a list of the people and situations that trigger a sense of self-doubt or a need to compete financially. How does it affect you when you feel you have to compete financially to prove your worth? Do you feel envy, anxiety, depression, stress, or anger around any of these issues? How would your feelings and behavior change if you let go of any tendency to equate your personal worth with your financial worth? How might you go about doing this, and what kind of support might you seek in the process?

2. Where has the culture's focus on money hurt you? Consider where you have suffered from the culture's over-focus on the pursuit of money. Are you feeling gouged by insurance companies and inadequate healthcare? Unable to get high quality food at decent prices? Threatened by toxins in your products? Chewed up by exorbitant bills for your children's education?

Cheated out of your nest egg by the stock market? How do you feel about ecological disasters afflicting the planet? How do you feel about the relationship of these ecological disasters to corporate exploitation of natural resources? These are all examples of social ills that result directly from both personal and corporate focus on financial profit, with minimal regard to other consequences. Are you willing to participate in a system that creates so much social abuse and physical destruction?

3. <u>Who do you admire?</u> Make a list of people you respect who may not make much money but seem to have a good spirit. Does one of your children's teachers invoke your respect? Your local body worker or massage therapist? Your children's sports coach? The forever cheerful cashier at the local supermarket? The kind and hardworking person who cleans your house? What can these people model for you, and what can you learn from them?

4. <u>Does financial fear affect your relationship to work?</u> Do you love your work? Do you feel respected? If not, are you feeling trapped because of financial pressures? If so, what small steps can you take to improve your situation? Can you break through any fears around asking for different responsibilities or a promotion? Can you confront negative behavior from colleagues with dignity and self-respect? Would it be useful for you at this time to seek out coaching to build your faith in yourself and your ability to confront demeaning situations at work? If you currently have no choice about where you work, what hobbies or community work can you do that feel like they come from your heart? How can you network with people who can help you brainstorm a new direction? Remember that big changes come from small steps.

5. <u>How does financial fear affect your intimate relationships?</u> Do you ever compromise yourself in your close relationships for the sake of financial benefit? Self-compromise can run the gamut all the way from not speaking up at times because of financial dependency, to getting into a relationship primarily for financial gain, to tolerating emotional or physical abuse for the sake of financial security. If you feel any of these hold true for yourself, how do you need to empower your voice in the relationship? What small steps can you take each day to gain greater financial autonomy? Do you need to reconsider your commitments to relationships that are more about money than they are about love? Think about where money affects your ability to be honest, open and independent in your relationships. What can you do to change this? Have you considered talking to a professional who might help you?

Crutch #2: The Roles We Play

The roles we assume in life—as dentist or engineer, housewife or lawyer, business person or actor—can be vehicles for effective self-expression. We can pour our love of life and passion for service into these roles. If you love your work, if you love sharing what you know and you bring caring to the people you work with, you are in the right place, using your role to manifest your internal sense of values. You probably don't judge or criticize much, and don't worry about others judging or criticizing you.

Unfortunately, while roles can be vehicles for authentic self-expression, they can also function as security blankets, feeding the need to be recognized, loved or powerful. There is a problem here: when we look to our roles to give us a sense of value, we also give away our power. Now we have to compete, perform, judge and be judged. Since our source of power ends up being outside us, in others' perception or in our status, we can never win. The role that looks like it can give us security instead ends up fueling insecurities.

Role Identity Creates the Compulsion to Judge

During my childhood and early adulthood, I was over-identified with my role. That made me a victim. Of course, the role I chose to play fit my deeper personality in certain respects. I had a natural metaphysical bent as a child, and so it was no accident that I eventually became a professor of philosophy, exploring existential questions about the meaning of life. Yet the values and behavior of my parents also strongly influenced how I expressed my innate interests. My parents were academics for whom intellectual achievement was supreme. I learned from them to identify my worth, my success and my lovability with my academic prowess. My brilliant intellectual performance and a long string of professional degrees were my security blanket. I graduated first among the women in my class at Harvard University, went to Cambridge University in England on a prestigious fellowship after graduating, and received a Ph.D. from Columbia University by the age of twenty-seven. I became a successful young professor, and my family was proud of me.

The gift to my life of an excellent academic education has been profound, and I am deeply grateful for the extraordinary blessings I received. Yet the problem for me was that even as I achieved, I based my sense of self on intellectual success in the eyes of the world. It took time for me to recognize that my interest in understanding what life was about was not necessarily compatible with the demands of intellectual brilliance, nor was it in line with the unwritten but powerful conventions of many academic institutions. Creativity and discovery are not always unequivocally welcome in the halls of academe. Like most professional institutions, academia is riddled with the competitiveness and backbiting that typify organizations where people evaluate their own worth by how they are perceived by colleagues and by management. The sacrosanct halls of learning sometimes teem with intellectual argumentation.

Unlike the corporate world, where money is king, in academia the power of the intellect represents the chief coin of value. It can be tempting to identify how good you are with how often you win an argument or prove someone else wrong. This is very different from being open to exploring and learning. Like some of my colleagues, I suffered from ego-based intellectual insecurities. I was not immune to the attractions of proving myself in intellectual fencing matches that were really about ego, not about the quest for understanding.

I gradually came to realize that the demands of academic achievement were in conflict with my need to understand myself and others more deeply. While another person might have been able to stay in university life and pursue a personally meaningful path, I could not. I had to let go of a role that I had learned to perform skillfully and to great applause in order to work on getting real.

In contrast to my highly applauded role as a professor, the profession I developed as a healer, body worker, author and teacher of self-healing was for many years completely marginalized by mainstream America. My parents were deeply concerned at my "failure" to live up to my "potential." Given the incredulity and skepticism of friends and family, I had to release myself from the temptation to evaluate myself on the basis of their opinions, and to trust that what I found to be true for myself would also be of value for others.

One of the biggest problems with relying on roles for a sense of security is that it makes us judgmental. We judge others by the standards of right and wrong that we associate with our role. Yet in doing so, we express our own insecurity, for there is no need to judge others unless we feel the need to protect ourselves. Why would you have to put others down unless to defend yourself? Why would you need to defend yourself unless you were already unsure of yourself? People who insist on their view of what is right have a brittle sense of themselves. If you know who you are, you do not have to impose your opinions. You can be as you are and let others be as they are.

The judgmental mind is the defensive ego's tool. No power is more punitive than the critical mind, and no power has greater ability to block accurate, objective and detached perception. When you focus on guaranteeing that you are right, you can find a reason to reject just about anything. You simply don't let in things that don't fit with your world view. This attitude makes a person narrow-minded, rigid and unpleasant to be around.

A simple exercise will show you that fear is the underlying and often unconscious source of the need to judge. When you next feel like arguing or judging someone else or yourself, pause for a moment and allow yourself to feel your body's sensations. You will probably notice tension: in your jaw, throat, neck, back or gut. You might also discover that your breathing has become somewhat constricted, another sign of tension. Tension is the voice of fear, of having to get it right, of having to be right, and of having to prove yourself right. The mind may tell you that what you are thinking is true, but the body tells you that you are reacting to fear.

The exercises below help identify where your professional and social roles are an appropriate expression of the true you, and where they function instead as an ego support that takes you away from your natural self. While these exercises are not solutions, they can assist you in identifying where you may be trapped, even if you don't think so, and help you take your next steps toward full empowerment.

Exercises: When roles don't serve you

1. Do you feel pressure to prove yourself? This is a manifestation of not feeling good enough. Are you relying on an outside credential to validate what can only be felt internally? Do you recognize any undercurrent of anxiety or of anger, accompanying a need to prove yourself? What might it feel like to

do what you do without needing to prove anything to anybody? Is it possible for you to detach from any need to prove yourself, even if only for a moment? Can you sense how liberating that can be, and how it increases your energy?

2. <u>Do you worry about others' criticism, or about being dismissed by others?</u> When others judge you this often expresses their own insecurity and need for power rather than an accurate evaluation of you. Think about people who judge you. Can you distinguish between feedback that is given from a place of love and criticism that is someone else's insecurity or rigidity foisting itself on you? Can you let go of reacting to criticism when it comes from someone else's lack of heart or their need to be right? What might this be like? Can you imagine yourself not reacting to the irritating criticism you receive from someone else?

3. <u>Do you ever criticize others for being different from you, or think that you are right and others are wrong?</u> What would it be like to be non-judgmental about others' points of view and lifestyle, no matter how different from your own? What do you gain by judging others? Is it worth the loss of connection and heart? Can you feel safe without having to judge? Do you need to judge in order to feel secure?

4. <u>Does achievement sometimes take first place over friendship, caring and collaboration?</u> How much do you want to make achievement and success a priority over the sense of community, love and self-nurturance? What do you gain and what do you lose when achievement comes first? How does the focus on achievement affect your ability to be in nurturing and supportive relationships?

5. <u>Do your roles reflect who you are?</u> If you feel your roles no longer fit you, you are at the beginning of

shifting what you do. You can mobilize this process of shifting by making lists of the following:

- Your skills
- Your passions
- What you felt like when you were at your best, and what you were doing
- What you want to learn
- Who you want to help
- What fears and modeling from your past are blocking you in finding a role more suitable for you (For example, are you following in your parents' footsteps; doing what you think others want you to do; doing what you do just for the money?).
- People you know who model the direction you want to go in, and with whom you can connect to help you move into the next phase of your life.

Making these lists starts you thinking about next steps. Consider talking to friends or to a coach to help you clarify a better direction for finding authentic self-expression in your life.

Crutch # 3: Living by Society's Rules

Rules keep things organized and predictable. We have a green light and a red light to manage traffic and to create a safe way to get across the street. Work schedules and procedures for running meetings help us get things accomplished and provide for the comforts of life. Recycling rules promote a more eco-friendly world. Societies that are law-abiding tend to be orderly, which supports everyone's wellbeing. Societies that are not law-abiding tend toward disorder, chaos and anarchy, which can harm everyone. Rules and regulations clearly help the social engine to function more smoothly.

Even the best rules can backfire in their original intent, however, if they keep us from thinking flexibly, creatively and with depth. The biggest problem lies with those rules that define what we consider to be "duty" and "obligation." These rules tell us, for example, to treat others with courtesy, to be kind to our parents, to do our duty by our children. All of this sounds good and reflects higher aspirations for humanity. The problem, however, is that when we identify our value with our obedience to these rules, the obedience can become a substitute for our quest for authenticity. When that happens, we validate ourselves by obeying the rules, rather than spontaneously doing what is right because it comes from our heart. The rules begin to control us. We begin to do things to conform: because we *have to* rather than because we *want to*.

Compulsive Dutifulness

Maria is the mother of three small children, is married to a kind, hardworking man and lives in a pleasant suburban neighborhood. While on the outside it looks like she has a perfect life, the truth is that Maria's plate is overloaded. She needs down time but she moves at a fast, anxiety-driven pace. She feels she has to meet all sorts of demands. On top of the family duties, she has to deal with the volunteering she is supposed to do at school, the charities she is supposed to help organize, the guests she is supposed to invite to her home on weekends, and the book club that it is her turn to organize. Then there are the acquaintances who want to drop by for coffee, people she can't turn away for fear of hurting their feelings. Of course, these are the same people who stay too long once they get in the door. Maria's life is crammed full of obligations that leave no room for anything else.

Maria feels that if she does not do all the things she is "supposed to do," she will be a bad person. The more she fills her life with obligations, the more she feels she is failing, since meeting all of these obligations makes her increasingly nervous. Anxious and frustrated at home and overburdened by responsibilities, she becomes irritable with her husband and children, and then accuses herself of being a poor mother, of not spending enough time with her children or her husband, and of being impatient. She is never good enough.

Even while Maria performs all her obligations, part of her feels it is all meaningless. She is right. It *is* meaningless because her obedience comes not from the heart but from self-criticism and a need to conform. Nonetheless, her friends and associates think she is an absolutely terrific mother and member of the community. After all, she contributes so much!

Maria is controlled by her super-ego, the harsh inner critic that constantly judges us, compelling us to do what we think we ought to do. Listening to her super-ego makes her nervous, competitive, anxious about social approval, conformist and sometimes resentful. What she wants is to be a good person. Yet being a good person is something that you are and not something that you do. Being good is a way of feeling—peaceful, contented and expansive—that gives birth to spontaneously generous ways of acting. Maria's super-ego is torturing her. Following her sense of obligation is not contributing to her peace of mind!

Maria has fallen victim to norms that encourage her to define her worth by what she does. This puts her on an endless treadmill. Now she can't just "be." She has a million things "to do" in order to be a good person. She becomes a human doing rather than a human being.

Maria needs to learn to let feeling peaceful take priority over doing what she thinks it is right to do. She needs to recognize that the constant monologue of self-criticism is a form of self-sabotage rather than a guide to being a good person. She makes herself tense and unhappy by listening to her inner critic, and her tension and unhappiness then render her less capable of bringing out her natural gifts and creating a peaceful and giving environment in her home.

Like all of us, Maria needs to let go of her inner critic. The first step in this process is simply to go on "Pause" when you hear your critic's voice. Let that voice talk away, but don't obey it just because it tells you that you should. The squeaky wheel doesn't always have to get the grease. Once you can do this, the second step is to give yourself enough space and time to release the constant stress of internal demands and to feel more relaxed. Having done this, you can proceed to the third step: asking yourself what feels right for you at this moment, not for anyone else, but for you. To listen to your own feelings, to listen to yourself rather than to someone else, is part of letting go of fear. Your head may fill your life with prescriptions and with things that you think you should do, but it is your own very personal feelings that provide effective guidance to what is right for you at any given time. When your head is filled with thoughts and prescriptions, it is hard to get in touch with how you feel, and how you feel is the only effective guide to what you should do.

Focusing on the Rules Stops You from Hearing and Feeling

Not only does our inner critic tend to keep us from getting in touch with and validating our feelings. Our sense of duty can so invade our life that it also blocks our ability to perceive accurately what is going on around us. In my classes, I do a simple experiment in communication that demonstrates this point.

First, I take participants through a meditative breathing exercise that helps them get more connected to their bodies and that quiets their inner dialogue. For five or ten minutes, they sit silently in a circle simply breathing and enjoying their sensations. Then I have the participants divide into groups of two. I tell them that each twosome is going to play a simple game. One person in the duo will listen to the other one for a few minutes without interrupting. Instead of engaging in conversation or commenting on what the other person is saying, the person who is listening will focus on gently observing her breathing, with the sole aim of being physically relaxed, peaceful and calm while listening. She is not to talk at all. This removes that person from having any responsibility for the conversation. Meanwhile, the person who is speaking is free to talk about anything at all: what she had for breakfast, a recent experience, family members or friends, the weather, and so on. After the groups of two do this for a few minutes, I have them change roles. The person who was listening while peacefully breathing gets to talk, and the person who was talking gets to focus on breathing in a relaxed manner while listening. Once this exercise is finished, we share our experiences. The sharing is invariably illuminating.

Virtually everyone who does this exercise is surprised to discover two interesting facts. First, when they practice listening in a relaxed way by following their breathing, they realize that they are usually somewhat nervous and tense when someone talks to them. It can be difficult for them to simply relax into listening! Instead, they feel compelled to take some kind of responsibility: to say something to the person they are listening to, to show that they are paying attention, to interject their own opinion, or to make the conversation lively. They realize that they have a compulsive need to talk that reflects anything from their concept of what it is to be a good conversationalist, to their need to reassure the other person or to inform them of their own opinion—anything and everything but just taking in what the other person is saying! This compulsiveness is about ego, about needing to fit in the way you think you should, and about needing to prove yourself or to be approved. It's about following social rules and not about being present.

The second fact class participants realize is that when they relax deeply into their breathing rather than acting out ego-dictated roles, they hear what the other person is saying at a much deeper level than they would have otherwise. The calmer they become, the better they hear. By giving up focusing on their own opinions or on saying the "right" thing in the conversation, they become better listeners. The people who talk during the exercise also recognize this and comment on how profound the experience of talking has been for them. In contrast to their experience in many conversations, they feel genuinely heard.

The key to effective communication lies not in doing various things to make the conversation move along or in establishing your own point of view, but in becoming quiet inside, so that you can actually absorb what the other person is saying. You give someone else your full attention by eliminating your own noise. If you can maintain inner quiet, you spontaneously say what is appropriate when the time comes for you to respond. You stop following rules or listening to ego and you absorb.

This exercise I take people through in classes is not a prescription for how to have a conversation under all circumstances. There are times when it can be important to say something to a speaker to help her clarify what she means, indicate that you are following her train of thought, and so on. The point of the exercise in quiet listening is that it makes the listener aware of how much ordinary conversational behavior is triggered by internal noise and by social rules, rather than by a genuine interest in hearing the other person. By directing the listener in this exercise to observe her own internal state, I give her an opportunity to clarify where she is being peaceful, and therefore capable of genuinely hearing, and where she is being reactive, and therefore not fully able to hear.

Rules can derail us, and abiding by them can sometimes literally tie us in knots. A number of years ago a woman appeared on my doorstep, walking with the help of crutches. Seven years prior, she had torn the meniscus in her left knee while skiing. Surgery and physical therapy had failed to resolve the problem. She had been to numerous doctors, therapists and healers, but had received little relief. She could not bend her leg. It was chronically swollen and became so hot at night that she had to sleep without covers on the left side of her body.

Despite seven years of being on and off crutches, the poor woman was determined to get well. She had a meticulous regimen of exercises that she completed each day. She actually scheduled every moment of her day, making sure that she never failed to do all the things that she thought she was supposed to do in order to heal.

Looking at how this woman moved and listening to what she said, I had a hunch about what might be contributing to her pain. From my training in bodywork and movement therapy, I knew that pain in any part of the body could be created or aggravated by tensions in other parts of the body. Knee problems such as this woman had are often related to chronic tensions in the pelvis, abdomen and low back. Soft, deep and relaxed breathing can help release some of these tensions. I therefore asked my client if she was familiar with using relaxed breathing for pain reduction, and she said yes, she knew how to breathe very slowly and deeply. I asked her to demonstrate this, and was astounded to observe what she then did. She did breathe very slowly and deeply, but with enormous tension! She worked very hard at breathing exactly as she thought she was supposed to breathe, putting significant effort into holding her breath in her abdomen for prolonged periods of time. Meanwhile, her body became rigid with the tension of the control she exerted. She was doing the opposite of what breathing was supposed to help her do—to release tension!

This is a good example of following a rule—in this case to breathe slowly and deeply—without any understanding of the original intent of the rule—in this case to release physical tension. By following her interpretation of the rule, my client created the opposite of the intended effect. She was oblivious of this, being so focused on doing things correctly that she paid no attention to how her body felt.

I gave the woman a simple lesson in breathing with less tension. Instead of following the rules as she understood them, she was to listen to and respond to her body's feedback so as to guide herself into breathing more softly and easily. Then I sent her home to practice. The next day, she told me with great excitement that she had more mobility in her leg than she had had for seven years. The moral? When we listen to the rules too much, we lose touch with our own feedback. We stop listening to ourselves.

To Say "Yes" You Have to be Able to Say "No"

Duties generally involve what we think of as our obligations toward others, as well as obligations we think others have toward us. Yet it is critical that we feel we have some choice about meeting what we call our duties. Not having choice is being a slave. Whatever we do willingly we must do from a place of choice. For this reason, the only way we can truly meet others' needs without harming ourselves, even when those needs are described as our duties, is if we are fully able to say "No" to others when that is the right choice for us. We have to feel inside that we are making a choice, not that we are being compelled. We have to be able to consider the possibility of not doing something as a prerequisite for possibly choosing to do it in a way that is both healthy and authentic. Being able to say "No" is a prerequisite for saying "Yes" genuinely and without self-damage. If you look at things this way, you can see what Maria's problem is. Maria, the suburban housewife and mother who is so burdened with family and social obligations, has not developed the ability to decide what is right for herself. She can't say "No," and therefore she can't say "Yes" and really mean it. She says "Yes" all the time, and she says it in response to what she experiences as pressure.

If doing something for someone else is not a free gift from your heart, it is destructive both to yourself and to others. It breeds self-avoidance, dependency, and what in Buddhism is called "attachment," the ultimate source of all suffering. Anything you do for the sake of the approval you get from others, or for the power you get over others, represents attachment. Attachment makes you unfree because when you are attached, in the sense that Buddhism uses that word, you need something from others in order to feel all right. That attachment is like a chain on your life. Once you are entangled in attachments, you are no longer free to choose. You are a slave, and those you serve are also your slaves, since you expect them to return the favor in some way.

Integrity, strength, and connection to your spiritual center require you to develop the strength of will and purpose that enable you to free yourself from defining your self-worth through your relationships. It is your will that enables you to identify your own independent source of direction. It is your will that helps you determine for yourself the difference between what social conventions tell you is right, and what you know is right for you.

Without a strong will, the offspring of courage, you are the puppet of your environment. Having a strong will (which is different from being willful) is having a good rudder with which to guide yourself toward your unique destiny in the currents of life.

In my own life, I had to struggle long and hard to identify an independent sense of direction. My demon was a very strong sense of obligation that I developed as a child, in particular my sense of obligation toward my mother. I had a wonderful mother. She did everything she could to raise her children well, especially after my parents' bitter divorce when I was nine. She sacrificed herself for her children. Needless to say, she had hard times, and because I was the closest to her of her three children, she often spoke to me of her troubles and confessed her depressions. I instinctively felt that she relied on me to lift her mood, and I internalized the sense that it was my "job" to stabilize her emotionally.

In my child-centered way, I did everything I could to support my mother, just as she did everything she could to support me. Yet because I was only a child, I also felt heavily burdened by my mother's depressions. It was only years later that I realized that my overwhelming sense of responsibility was partly based on a childhood fear that my mother would suffer a mental collapse and that we children, having already lost our father, would be left without our mother as well. As is often the case with children, my sense of obligation to my mother was founded in part on my own survival needs. I was desperate to support my mother because without her I would be lost.

Growing up with a heavy sense of responsibility fosters ambivalence. As I matured, I became increasingly aware of this. I loved my mother and understood that she relied on me to meet her emotional needs, but I also resented having to be there for her. As a result I performed my duties ambivalently. My critical mind chastised me for my ambivalence, but that self-criticism was just another weight on me. What is the point of telling yourself you should feel differently from the way you feel? That is just self-hatred at work. You are what you are, and you feel how you feel, and that is how it should be because that is how it is. This does not mean that how we feel at any given time is its own justification, and that we should all go around in the world proudly proclaiming our hatreds, jealousies and frustrations. What it does mean is that becoming healthier starts with accepting how we feel rather than rejecting it. After all, what we don't accept in ourselves stays with us. Self-acceptance is both a first step to effective change, and a step in granting ourselves the self-love which is the foundation for love of others. You cannot become a more whole person without being a more self-loving person. Most of our limitations, including for me the negative feelings I once held toward my mother, reflect a lack of faith in ourselves.

I began to solve the dilemma of ambivalence toward my mother when I decided that my goal was no longer to be a good person or a person with right on her side, but rather to be a person at peace. I decided that instead of directing my behavior toward my mother by listening to the critical super-ego in my head, a super-ego that tortured me with the constant obligations it imposed on me, I would make my decisions moment by moment on the basis of what helped me to feel more peaceful. I traded in the demands of obligation in favor of listening to the call of inner tranquility.

When I decided on peace over duty, I made a choice familiar to the thinking of many Eastern spiritual traditions that recognize peace as the foundation of all personal and social healing. They also know that peace is not simply an emotional and mental state. It is also deeply physical. It is not possible to feel mentally or emotionally at ease without also feeling physically at ease. Physical tranquility and mental/emotional tranquility are one and the same. Eastern traditions therefore emphasize physical relaxation and tension release as important steps toward greater self-awareness and emotional self-mastery. In my own stumbling toward self-growth, I somehow recognized this and decided to respond to my mother at any given moment on the basis of whatever helped me to feel more *physically relaxed*. Little did I know then that I was taking a significant turn in the road that would lead me both toward greater personal authenticity and toward a greater capacity for love. Taking the road of peace rather than the road of duty was going to make me a better person, not only with myself but also with others.

When my mother would call or tell me she wanted something of me, I would notice how my body felt at the time. Sometimes my neck or chest would tighten up. When that happened, her requests were triggering tension in me, and the tension reflected my internal conflict. My mind was telling me I ought to do what my mother wanted, but my body was rebelling and telling me that her requests felt like impositions that I was afraid of refusing. Obeying my super-ego would be giving in to my fear of displeasing my mother, and trying to meet her needs because of my fear. I realized, however, that the best path for me would be not to respond to fear. Therefore, whenever I felt tense in communications with my mother, I would apologize as gently as I could and back away from whatever she wanted. I practiced letting go of the compulsion to be a good girl. I did what I needed to do to help my body feel more peaceful in as tactful a way as I could at the moment.

Over time I was able to be more consistently physically relaxed and calm in my mother's presence because I was giving myself the right to do what was right for me rather than what she wanted. I was less duty-bound. This made me more loving with my mother when I did spend time with her. When I helped her, I did so with less ambivalence and a bigger heart. When I did not, it was because this was the honest thing for me to do at the time. Because I could say "No" to my mother's requests when I needed to, I didn't feel controlled by her. And once I wasn't controlled by my perception of her needs, I could more freely and genuinely say "Yes." I also found myself saying "Yes" more often. Letting go of compulsion helped me to find my heart, and finding my heart helped me to give freely what I had once given begrudgingly as a duty.

Having the ability to say "No" implies that when you say "Yes" you really mean it. That is authenticity and personal power. Similarly, being unable to say "No" implies that when you say

"Yes," you do so out of fear and with resentment instead of out of strength and commitment. You give away your power.

Duty lives in us as an inner critic. As a healthcare practitioner, I see countless people who suffer chronic pain as a result of their inability to let go of their inner critic. They cannot allow themselves to deviate from what they have learned they should do, so as to be able to do what they really want to do. They live in a state of ambivalence and resentment, classic signs of conflict that over the long term deplete us so much that we can become ill. It takes courage and plenty of practice to identify what is right for us, no matter what others think. Owning this ability is an essential ingredient of physical as well as emotional and mental healing.

The great religions of the world originated as calls to let go of social and moral conformism in order to develop a strong center that knows what is right for us personally. There is nothing conformist or submissive about true spirituality. For example, Christ's commandment not to resist evil and to turn the other cheek when struck has nothing to do with being submissive. The person who can literally turn the other cheek is the person who chooses not to react to another's abuse, not the person who cannot defend himself and who lacks courage. Similarly, the Dalai Lama chose not to resist evil in Tibet, and he did this not from weakness but from strength. That is what makes his message so powerful.

Duty, Slavery and the Inner Life

When the sense of duty is not grounded in a strong sense of personal integrity and self-love it is destructive to our personal growth, to self-inquiry, and to an authentic sense of community. The monk Vivekananda says this in scorching terms:

> Duty becomes a disease with us; it drags us on for ever. It catches hold of us and makes our whole life miserable. It is the bane of human life. This duty, this idea of duty, is the midday summer sun, which scorches the innermost soul of mankind. Look at those poor slaves to duty! Duty leaves them no time to say

prayers, no time to bathe; duty is ever on them. They go out and work; duty is on them. They come home and think of the work for the next day; duty is on them. It is living a slave's life and at last dropping down in the street and dying in the harness, like a horse. This is duty as it is understood...what is this duty after all? It is really attachment—the impulsion of flesh. And when an attachment has become established we call it duty....When attachment becomes chronic, we baptize it with the high sounding name of duty.... There is no duty for you and me. Whatever you have to give to the world do give by all means, but not as duty....Everything that you do under compulsion goes to build up attachment.[3]

Many of the world's great spiritual leaders abandoned what others viewed as their duties in society and exhorted others to do the same. Jesus called upon his devotees to let go of mother, father and family and to follow him. Buddha, born as a prince into a wealthy family, abandoned both the wealth of his position and its duties to find self-realization. Ramakrishna was a nineteenth-century Hindu seeker after God who is widely recognized in India as having a spiritual stature equivalent to that of Christ in the West. For years Ramakrishna was viewed as insane by those around him because of his strange behavior and his complete disregard for social convention. Only when the depth of his self-realization was recognized did he begin to be seen as an extraordinarily advanced spiritual being whose indifference to social convention was in his case a manifestation of spiritual enlightenment.

Living authentically does not require us to defy the social order or to be a rebel. In fact, defiance and rebelliousness are only signs of our attachment to what we claim to reject. What living authentically does require is for us to make our first priority finding our own truth rather than relying for our sense of self-worth on following the moral codes dominant in our society.

---

3   Vivekananda, "Karma Yoga" (*op. cit.*), p. 500

Defining our self-worth by reliance on those codes is mental and emotional slavery, the opposite of self-empowerment and self-realization. That slavery only hurts us, and when we follow moral codes without being fully grounded in ourselves, we can't avoid becoming insecure, anxious, resentful, and judgmental even while we are trying to be good. Being able truly to love and care for others depends on being able truly to love ourselves.

The exercises below serve as tools for letting go of too great a focus on rules and obligations as vehicles for self-validation. They aim to help you create more heart in your life.

Exercises: Replace obligations with heart

1. <u>Eliminate "ought" and "should" from your motivational scheme.</u> Notice how often you tell yourself that you "ought" to do something or that you "should" do it. These words indicate a possible conflict between what you really want to do and what your super-ego is telling you to do. Go on "Pause" when you hear that voice in your head telling you what you should do, and ask yourself what you really want to do. Make sure that you can honestly say to yourself that what you do is what you want to do, not just what you should do.

2. <u>Refrain from using "ought" and "should" as ways to get others to do things.</u> Notice how often you tell others what you think they "ought" to do. Recognize that this can involve using moral coercion rather than loving discourse. No one likes to be told what they should do, and if someone responds to this kind of language, they do this out of fear. That is harmful to them and to you. If you think that it would be a good idea for someone else to do something, clarify for them why it would help them by replacing moral verbiage with rational persuasion.

3. <u>Do you have trouble saying "No?"</u> If you have trouble saying "No" to requests from others in your

relationships, at work, or in your social life, you will find yourself sometimes feeling stressed, pressured, and unhappy or conflicted when you say "Yes." See if you can notice when you feel this pressure, and practice saying "No"—diplomatically and gently if possible, but also clearly and firmly. This will help you to say "Yes," when you do so, with greater commitment.

Summary

Carl Jung, the eminent founder of depth-consciousness psychology, described the first thirty years of life as a process of socialization, and the rest of life as a process of individuation. In your early years, you learn to abide by the rules, to do things the way you are told, to identify success by other people's norms, and to succeed in other people's terms. In your mature years, you face the challenge of learning to undo all of that: to let go of being society's child and to become yourself. This chapter has explored the three main ways our culture has of turning us into obedient servants of the social machine: by endorsing materialism, consumption and financial power; by encouraging us to identify ourselves with our professional and social roles; and by inculcating in us specific rules and codes of conduct that become aspects of our super-egos.

Following these three types of cultural precepts cannot give us what we really need. It is the desire for security and freedom from fear that motivate us to live by codes imposed from outside. We say to ourselves that if we can earn enough, if we can be successful enough, if we can be "good" enough, then perhaps we will be safe, secure and loved. Yet the quest for security founded on outer symbols ends up taking us further away from our inner source of serenity and power rather than toward it. Our reliance for a sense of security on money or consumption, on prestige or on doing the right thing eventually contributes to increasing anxiety, fear, anger, depression, resentment, and all the other negative emotions that make life difficult. Since it is negative emotions that drive people to look for security in the first place, seeking external validation of our inner worth only puts us in a vicious cycle of mental, emotional and physical suffering.

The path to finding contentment, true success, an open heart and personal power is an inner path and requires an inner healing. We have to take our attention away from outer symbols of success, look at our own inner state, and fight the victory battle on our own turf: inside ourselves. The more we master our internal state, the more we become not only increasingly happy and at peace, but also increasingly successful outwardly. In the end, we are far more likely to achieve richly in the outer world if we turn our focus to where it should be, on our inner world and inner healing. By mastering the chaos of our inner worlds, we also master the chaos of our outer world. These topics, forming the steps to freedom, to self-liberation, and to our personal destiny, form the subject of Part II.

PART II
The Solution

3

Taming Your Mind

**To be calmly active and actively calm—a Prince of Peace
sitting on the throne of poise, directing the kingdom of
activity—is to be spiritually healthy.**
- Yogananda, *SRF Lessons*

Finding our way to feeling both empowered and peaceful involves
realizing that there is one thing and one thing only that we have to
make a top priority. We have to work on managing and mastering
what's going on inside us. It's our internal state that is the problem,
and our internal state that we have to transform. Relying on
anything outside us to make us happy just doesn't work in the
end.

Possessions, people and events come and go, but you take your
internal state with you wherever you go. Your journey to freedom
begins when you recognize the need to cultivate inner calm and
personal empowerment by figuring out how to take charge of
your own internal landscape, no matter what is happening on the
outside. Doing this isn't just the foundation of a spiritual life. It's
the foundation of a happy, successful and free life.

You can't necessarily control external events, but you can
definitely learn to control how you react to them. The more you
do that, the more you also find that mastering your internal state
and your reactions helps you influence the outside world. That's
two benefits for the price of one!

A strong and peaceful center gives you a powerful ally for navigating the tides of life. I remember the very first time I clearly experienced this truth. It was one morning when I was able for the first time to shift my anxious and angry reactions to an abusive employer. I figured out how to be relaxed and detached, regardless of what he said. He was the same person who had so often made me miserable, but I was different. I felt liberated! And there was an added bonus. Unconsciously influenced by the subtle change within myself, my employer began to treat me with greater respect.

When you learn how to take charge of your inner state, and you make that more important than reacting to external events, you begin to eradicate your mental and emotional restlessness, confusion, depression, anxiety, fear, worry, anger and other uncomfortable feelings. You don't have to go into a cave or become a hermit; you can stay fully active in your daily affairs. Rather, instead of being jerked around by life, you use events, including unpleasant ones, to observe how you react, and to develop tools for becoming calmer. Along the way, you become clearer about how much your own mind is creating your problems, and as you practice transforming self-destructive mental patterns, you grow into your personal power. Mastering outer reality happens easily enough if you can first master internal reality. Going the other way doesn't relieve the human dis-ease. The steps in the journey of self-mastery are simple, systematic and powerful. Let's lay them out.

Step 1: Observe Your Demon Mind

The first step is to observe your own mind in action. What goes on in your mind while you are busy paying attention to what you want to have and what you have to do? If you're like the vast majority of people, the answer is obvious: your mind just runs on and on. It never stops talking. It's a radio tuned to its own channel, renting space in your head, jumping from one thought or feeling to the next, dragging you in its train.

How often have you lain in bed at night unable to sleep because of all the thoughts passing through your head? How often do you wake up in the morning talking to yourself about everything you have to do that day, or caught up in confusion about what to do next? How often do you find yourself working on one project while thinking about the next one? Or running a program in your mind while someone else is talking to you? You are witnessing the restless, compulsive activity of your mind, the activity that Buddhist traditions recognize as the primary problem of the human condition.

When you start observing your thoughts, you recognize that some are random, and some are fragments of memories. Others are obsessive; they go over and over the same issue. Still others play out a future event, or endlessly analyze some past event. Some thoughts have a temporary pleasure attached to them, but many are not particularly pleasant. Most are distracting, if not downright exhausting. Having your mind chattering away is like being on hold on the telephone, forced to listen to music that you intensely dislike playing in the background. If only it would stop!

A lot of us put time and energy into escaping our mental chatter. Television is a terrific self-hypnotic tool: you substitute the non-stop talk of the television for the non-stop talk of your mind. Having a drink or a cigarette, taking a tranquilizer or a sleeping pill, calling or texting someone for distraction, socializing whenever restlessness hits, these are all tools we frequently use to avoid dealing with internal noise. They're not effective. The more we react to inner chatter by seeking distraction, the more the chatter grows.

Mental chatter is the bubonic plague of the mind, a plague fostered and aggravated by a culture and educational system that overvalue left-brain linear thinking and accumulation of information, and that undervalue personal experience. It's personal experience, and not what other people tell us, that over time teaches us how to develop our real intelligence and judgment. If we don't learn to trust our own perceptions, we get overtaken by second-hand knowledge and never learn to figure things out for ourselves.

Our educational system has its merits, but its approach to learning over-emphasizes the digestion of information given to us by others. This can hamstring our independence and creative capacities, not to speak of our inner balance. It's no accident that modern education has this bias. It developed during industrialization as a response to the need for workers to man the lines of the industrial machine. It focused not on teaching self-awareness, creativity or growth, but on getting students to master repetitive tasks and assimilate information relevant to performing specific skills. This makes for a lot of internal monologue and not too much self-knowledge. Constant thinking and analyzing cripple the freedom of the mind by creating a garbage dump of mental chatter inside us.

Some people make the mistake of calling their mental chatter "thinking." Yet this chatter is far from true thought, which is creative and open. It is closer to an obsession with control. The first signs of mental chatter originate in the primitive survival strategies we develop as children in the face of what seems to be an unsafe world. No matter how nurturing our infancy, the experience of being a baby and then a child necessarily includes a profound sense of vulnerability and need for security. As children we depend on others for the satisfaction of our basic needs, and that is where our mental chatter begins.

When first born, we just feel what we feel and express what we express. We don't monitor. Then there comes a time when we figure out that we need to monitor and control. We let go of purely experiencing, and begin to "think" or strategize as we come to grips with the fact that the world outside us controls our wellbeing. Our "thinking" is an effort to control in return, whether by controlling ourselves or controlling others.

When I was three years old sitting on my daddy's knee, dying to bounce up and down, I quickly learned the difference between a spontaneous expression of my own spirit and the demands of my environment. I realized from my father's behavior that a condition of being allowed to stay on his knee was to be quiet. I suppressed my urge to bounce around for the sake of an outer reward. I strategized. I thought. This was a simple enough experience, and not particularly traumatic. But it demonstrates how mental chatter starts with the suppression of immediate feelings and perceptions, replaced by the need to control. Over time, that need to control can turn into a monster inside our heads that removes us more and more from who we really are, what we really feel, and how we innately experience our world. Returning to our original state is returning to being present. Ironically, learning to be present makes having to think about things irrelevant. When we are present we know immediately what we have to do. When we need to control ourselves or others, rather than be present, we have to "think." Welcome to the inner demon that directs your life, that radio channel in your head making constant commentaries and evaluations.

Mental chatter makes for tension. Have you ever noticed that you feel tense when your mind starts talking? It is a scientific fact that physical tension accompanies mental chatter. The more you listen to your mental chatter, the more you feel tense. The more you feel tense, the more you think and the harder it is to find peace. Anyone who goes on a beautiful vacation and finds himself unable to relax has experienced this fact. There you are in the perfect setting for letting go, and you find you can't. Your mind just races on.

Mental chatter makes us unintelligent relative to our true potential. I once gave a workshop on optimal performance to women CEOs. I asked each person to recall when they had experienced their last creative inspiration. Every single person answered that it was at a time when they were *not thinking.* For one person, it was standing in the shower while washing her hair; for another it was taking a beautiful walk in the country; for another, it was after a long peaceful day reading a book at home. All the participants acknowledged that when their minds were occupied with thoughts, they didn't function at a high level. It was when their minds were empty that things began happening.

Mental chatter or "thinking" is an aspect of the limited, conscious mind. Creative processes come from the non-conscious mind.

If you don't realize that mental chatter is nothing more than anxiety and the need to control, you fall into the trap of giving it credibility. You wake up in the middle of the night and spend two hours sleeplessly thinking about how to solve that problem you encountered at work, or how to deal with that person who offended you.

You are more intelligent when you don't think. You find solutions more easily if you think less. Knowing this helps you to detach from the demon mind. That is a step in the right direction.

To move toward less chatter and more presence, explore the following suggestion.

Exercise: Observe your mental chatter

Notice what is going on in your mind. Put down whatever you are doing, close the door and turn off the computer and the telephone. Stop doing anything. Who is talking inside your head? What is the tone of voice? What is it saying to you? Is it friendly or critical, irritating or soothing? Are you hearing random fragments? Is your mind going over lists of things to do? Is it going over and over some issue you are dealing with? How much of your attention gets absorbed by your internal monologue? How does your body feel? Does it feel relaxed and soft, or does it feel tight or numb?

Since most people fall fairly easily into obsessive thinking patterns, especially under stress, this is a good exercise to do periodically to remind yourself that the voice inside your head is neither helpful nor pleasurable. You might also want to notice what thought patterns tend to repeat themselves over and over. These represent habits of mind that are destructive to your wellbeing.

Step 2: Choose Peace

How much you manage to master the restless and obsessive mental chatter of your mind depends on how you answer one pivotal question: How much do you want inner peace? Most of us certainly want inner peace, yet are we willing to do the work of taming and training the mind so as to attain it? If we are, do we know what that work involves?

Inner peace is beautiful, proud and independent. She needs to be won. If you want her, you have to make getting her your *number one priority*, something that you will not sacrifice pursuing for *anything*, no matter how tempting. That's a process that involves each of us using this moment, the next moment, and the one after that as opportunities to do battle with whatever makes us nervous, upset, angry, or restless. We don't have to win each battle, and we don't have to find all the peace we want right away. We can take our time, and we can take all the time we need. But we do have to commit the time we have to pursuing that goal. Becoming more peaceful requires confronting our addiction to internal chatter. That's a daily practice. When we commit to inner peace, we learn to use every situation in life, whether pleasant or unpleasant, as a tool for developing and strengthening our inner poise, strength and calm.

Exercise: Practice choosing peace

1. Write down whatever makes you nervous, upset, agitated, irritated or angry. Among the things that many people find irritating or upsetting are: being late for an event or for work; having someone disagree with you, or disagreeing with someone else; feeling you don't look your best; having someone yell at you or treat you dishonestly; failing to meet someone else's expectations, or someone else failing to meet

your expectations; being put on hold on the telephone for a long time.

2. <u>Notice the pain you experience from losing inner peace.</u> After you have written down your list, ask yourself if you can recognize that being upset, nervous or angry hurts you, even if the situation that triggers these feelings is not pleasant. Can you imagine dealing with whatever the situation might be from a more balanced place—a place that is calmer and less reactive? Below is a simple way to practice doing that. In addition, if you would like audio support for this exercise, you can download the MP3 *Empowering Your Intention* from my website, www.ingridbacci. com. Alternatively, you can listen to this and other exercises for developing inner peace by downloading my entire exercise series called *Effortless Practice,* available either as CDs or as MP3s.

3. <u>Relax deeply for a few moments by observing the rhythm of your breathing.</u> When you are ready, imagine the situation that makes you nervous or upset. See the person or situation as clearly as you can, hear the tones of voice and other sounds. You are running a movie of the situation in your mind. Does your body shift out of its relaxed state into a more agitated one? Now let go of what you imagined, and just breathe quietly for a few moments until you are calm again. Then try to imagine seeing yourself in the same situation looking, acting and feeling balanced, poised and calm. Can you use your imagination to shift your automatic reaction to the situation? If it is difficult for you to do this, you can imagine someone else in that situation, perhaps someone whom you admire, looking and acting calm and poised. Then imagine that you are that person. See yourself (or imagine being that person) dealing with the situation in a balanced, empowered manner, no matter what happens. You are practicing letting

go of internal automatic reactions of agitation, and replacing them with empowered feelings of peace. Repeat this exercise on a regular basis, and then recall it when you are in the actual situation that bothers you, so as to help you shift your behavior. Rehearsal makes for good performance!

Step 3: Meditate to Calm Your Mind

Anything you don't react to eventually goes away. If someone you don't want to speak to calls you incessantly and you don't pick up the phone, that person will finally stop calling. If a friend has a habit of trying to get your attention by complaining, and you don't react to the complaints but let them pass without comment, your friend will one day cease complaining. If your mind runs on and on, jumping and screaming and yelling or obsessing, and you watch without reacting, it will gradually quiet down.

Watching your mind without reacting is a meditative practice called witnessing. Witnessing develops a sense of being separate from our mental chatter. That helps us become calmer, staying detached from the radio static in the background of our lives.

Jon Kabat-Zinn, who in the 1990s introduced meditation as a healing modality into hospital clinics in the United States, describes meditation as focusing your attention on purpose. In meditation, you deliberately focus your attention on a single thing—a mantra, concept, or physical sensation like the breath—and maintain that focus in order to separate yourself from your internal monologue.

Focusing your attention on purpose is no easy task. Beginning meditators can feel restless, bored or sleepy within a few minutes of starting to meditate. It takes patient practice to gradually improve your focus and your ability to be still. The rewards are well worth the effort. Experiencing inner stillness is deeply relaxing, which explains why people who have practiced inner arts for a long time seem to be happy. They are. They have let go of internal agitation.

In my classes, I have students focus on gently observing their breathing when they meditate. This form of meditation is called *Vipassana*. There are numerous approaches to meditation, but meditating by observing the breath has three distinct benefits, the combination of which make it superior as a tool for empowering your life:

First, like other forms of meditation, focusing on experiencing the sensation of your breath gives you an *anchor* for your awareness that helps you detach from your mind's noise. Whenever you notice yourself getting involved in your thoughts, you come back to focusing your attention on gently feeling your breathing.

Second, focusing on the breath is physiologically relaxing, and this creates greater mental and emotional calm.

Third, and most important, once you have learned through meditative breathing in a quiet space to feel calmer, you can use this tool anywhere and anytime, with transformative effects in your daily life. You can focus on your breathing while cooking, doing laundry, riding on the train or driving the car to work, meeting deadlines, and handling an argument with a family member, friend or colleague. Each time you do this, you become less reactive, more peaceful in the moment, and better able to address a situation proactively and constructively.

Because focusing on your breath can be practiced anywhere, it gives you a tool that helps you every moment of your life for the rest of your life. This is not true of other meditative centering tools such as focusing on a mantra or a concept. For example, if you focus on a mantra or a concept while you are having a conversation, you won't hear the person you are talking to very well. If you focus on your breathing, however, you will hear them even better than otherwise because you are inducing in yourself a state of deepened relaxation and an empty mind. The exercise at the end of this section shows you how to practice meditation on the breath.

Mental habits of judgment can intrude on your meditation and should be ignored. Let's say that as you're meditating, you say to yourself, "I can't do this," or "This is stupid," or "What a horrible thought I just had," or "I wish I weren't so restless." You are judging yourself, something the mind likes to do. But judging is just another way of getting back into mental chatter. When you start making judgments, you activate the mind chatter you want to get rid of.

Let's say you have an angry thought. You go into judgment if you react to it either by being angry at yourself for feeling that way or by being angry at the person or situation you blame for the thought. Let's say you have a depressing thought. You go into judgment if you react to it by thinking of all the reasons you are depressed, who or what caused your depression, how to solve it, and so on. Judgment involves reacting to a thought or feeling that comes into your mind by having other thoughts and feelings. Non-judgment involves noticing thoughts and feelings in the same way that you might notice the clouds passing through the sky: with interest but without reaction.

Things go better for you when you don't judge. It's kinder to yourself and more efficient. Imagine two people who are having an argument. Usually each party wants to be right and neither party wants to listen to the other. They just create garbage between them. Not reacting to one another is much cleaner. If one person decides not to argue with the other, but just listens until there is space to calmly express his views, chances are that both persons will come to understand each other better. Your relationship with your own thoughts is analogous. If you stop judging or reacting to your own thoughts and instead let them come up and pass through, you feel better. By being more accepting, you release the mental garbage more quickly.

Practicing meditation can raise buried emotions. A client named Ahmed suffered mental confusion and back pain. His mind was a pit of endless drifting and repetitive thoughts. After one of our sessions, I gave him a meditation CD to take home and listen to daily. The next week, he reported a significant realization. As his mental chatter and mind wandering diminished during meditation, he was able to notice what was going on inside. He realized that he had anxiety of which he had not previously been aware, and that his constant thinking and confusion were masks that hid this anxiety from view. As he continued to meditate over the next few weeks, his anxiety gradually decreased, along with his mental chatter.

What Ahmed discovered about himself is true of all of us who experience mental chatter. Underneath the chatter are unrecognized emotions. The chatter enables us to avoid the emotions. Calming the mind reveals your subconscious patterns and helps you heal. It can be difficult to stay with meditation when painful feelings come up, but doing so allows you to acknowledge those feelings that have been suppressed. When you acknowledge what has been suppressed, that allows for release. Just as a food craving will stop being so persistent if you notice it but neither feed it nor repress it, so, too, painful emotions will dissolve when you allow them to be there without trying to do something about them.

Exercise: Practice meditative awareness

You can obtain an expanded audio version of the following meditation exercise on my website, www. ingridbacci.com, as an individual *Meditation* MP3 or as part of the series of exercises in self-calming and self-healing, entitled *Effortless Practice,* and available as a CD or as an MP3.

1. Find a quiet place where you can sit or lie down without interruption, for between five and twenty minutes. Focus gently on your intention of finding greater peace. To help you do this, imagine something that gives you a profound sense of stillness: a beautiful scene from nature or a wonderfully peaceful memory. Absorb yourself in this image or memory until you can feel yourself becoming increasingly still.

2. Now let go of the image and gently scan your body with your attention. Start with your feet, then your ankles, calves and thighs, absorbing how they feel. Don't try to change anything. Simply experience how

you are right now. Continue doing this slowly and gently, moving up through your pelvis, abdomen, rib cage, shoulders and neck, down your arms, and then to your face. Imagine being soft. Notice and accept how the sensation of your body has changed.

3. Once you are fully present to your body, let your attention shift to the sensation of your breath as it moves in and out of your body. Absorb yourself in the wavelike sensation of the breath. Watch your breath without trying to change it in any way, and when you find your mind drifting, gently bring your attention back to being anchored in the feeling of the breath. Your body and mind will gradually become quieter.

4. After you have quietly watched your breathing for a while, imagine it is like a caress. Each wave of the breath reaches into you softly, inviting you to open and feel yourself more deeply. Imagine that the breath is moving more and more deeply into your body, until it fills your pelvis and then your entire torso. Do not try to make the breath go deeper. Simply imagine, and your body will find its way into further softening, letting go, and stillness. Enjoy experiencing the feeling of open, expansive breathing for as long as you like.

5. When you are ready to come to the close of your meditation, open your eyes. Maintain some awareness of the breath as you look around the room. Notice that this helps you maintain a sense of internal quietness. Let yourself recall and live in that internal quietness during the day.

Step 4: Be Present

Picture a man with an attaché case walking through a beautiful city park. It is spring, the sun is shining, birds are out, and flowers are everywhere. The man is bent over, deep in thought as he walks along. There is a mushroom-shaped black cloud of thought over his head. His awareness is in the black cloud, not in the beauty of the world around him. He is in his mind chatter.

The reward of observing your mind without reacting to its chatter is the gift of being more present to your life. You can show up for what is happening.

Years ago I had a revealing experience that taught me this lesson. I was new to the healing path, and had asked a gifted psychic to teach me how to be more intuitive. I thought she was going to give me a fancy meditation, train me to see auras or tell me how to channel spirits. She was going to show me something exotic! Instead, she suggested to me that the next time I went to my local post office, I might spend a little time observing the clerk behind the counter.

When I next went to the post office, I realized that my psychic friend had indirectly counseled me to think less and be more present. I also realized that I had never really engaged with the clerk behind the counter. He had been just another human cipher I dealt with in the process of getting my tasks done. After that day, I enjoyed talking to this gentleman whenever I visited the post office. I was more present. Over the years I also realized that the more present we are, the more intuitive we are. Intuition is a natural consequence of learning to be present. When we are present, we have an empty mind, a mind that, because it is uncluttered, can be open, receptive and curious.

You are present when you let go of thinking. If you are having a conversation with someone, and you are thinking about what you want to say next, then you have difficulty hearing that person and appreciating their unique point of view. You also have difficulty responding spontaneously and creatively. You are stuck in your mental chatter. You are not present. If you are on the golf course or playing tennis, and you are thinking about your next move, or about how well or badly you are doing, you have difficulty performing optimally. Letting go of thinking enriches your life and makes you more effective.

You can either think or experience. You can't do both. Being present is experiencing being in flow. Whether it's in playing a game of golf or tennis, having a deep conversation, being fully engrossed in a project, or making love, flow moments are characterized by the absence of thought. Things just happen. Learning how to be present is letting your life happen through you.

Exercise: Practice being present

Take five minutes each day to practice being present. See if you can take in what is around you without thinking about it. The easiest way to do this is to focus your attention on observing your sensations: how your body feels, what you are hearing and seeing, smelling and tasting, without judgment. You might also want to sit and listen to the sounds around you. Look outside and absorb the colors and shapes. Alternatively, if you are looking at someone, see if you can just absorb the way they look and sound with curiosity and without judgment. If you are exercising, be fully present to the sensations of your body. How do your legs, arms, shoulders and neck feel? What is it like to observe without trying to change anything? Notice how rich everything becomes when you do this, and how much more focused you are.

Step 5: Center Yourself

If you can tame your mind and become still, like the eye at the center of a storm, you develop enormous power in the face of life's vicissitudes. The more you increase your inner quiet, the more powerful your focus and your energy become. The eminent author George Bernard Shaw once said that he saw his life as a brightly burning flame whose goal was to continue to burn strong and bright to the very end. He was a prolific and gifted man who blessed the world with his creations. He was centered and focused within himself. Most people lack this kind of focus: they are like flickering, intermittent flames, with very little staying power. We all owe it ourselves to become brightly burning flames.

I have heard people say that they would probably have better focus if only they could find their purpose. They think that focus is a consequence of having purpose. The truth is the opposite. If you do not develop effective powers of focus, you cannot identify a true sense of purpose, let alone pursue it. You need to be able to focus your attention clearly and at will in order to be able to identify meaningful purposes that you wish to pursue. Once you have identified those purposes, their pursuit further strengthens your power of focus, but without the initial ability to train your attention, purpose cannot emerge into view. Your mind is too distracted.

Whenever your mind is reactive, your focus gets scattered. Let's say you don't receive an email when you expect it, and you become irritated or depressed. That is the mind's reactivity at work. You lose control over your inner state. Let's say your flight connection is delayed and you spend hours at the airport worrying about your next connection. That is the mind's reactivity at work, and for you that equals wasted time, not at the airport, but in the home of your mind. Let's say an employer or colleague doesn't respond the way you had hoped, and you spend all night trying to figure out how to get him to change his mind. That is the mind's reactivity at work, exhausting you and draining you of your creative potential. Alternatively, that colleague or employee responds the way you had hoped, and now this has made your day, so you shout and dance for joy. That too is the mind's reactivity at work. The extent to which a small trigger can make you joyful is also the extent to which a small trigger can make you depressed. Both demonstrate the mind's lack of center.

The more easily events affect you, whether positively or negatively, the more reactive you are. The stronger your center, the more you are able to maintain an even keel, regardless of events. Being able to maintain an even keel has a visible energetic dimension of radiant aliveness and energy. Centered people burn brightly and are highly effective. They also give abundantly. They share their energy.

Have you ever been exhausted after spending time in someone's presence? Energetically exhausting people have no center. Often, they have focused for so long on doing what they think must be right or on getting others' approval that they have little sense of themselves. Their mental over-activity also makes them susceptible to mental diseases of aging like Alzheimer's and senility. Studies of older members of monastic orders reveal that they have much lower levels of Alzheimer's and senility than the average population. This is probably a result of their regular practice of disciplines like prayer and meditation, a practice that gives them strong powers of focus.

Exercise: Practice centering

The following simple exercise develops your power to center yourself. Draw a large black dot in the center of a blank sheet of paper. Hold it in front of you or pin it up on a wall, and sit or stand in front of it. Breathing in a relaxed way, focus your attention on the black dot. Notice how often your attention wanders. Do this daily for several minutes at a time to enhance your powers of focus.

Step 6: Concentrate Effortlessly

There is a science to focusing your energy and becoming a channel for inspiration. The ancient system of Raja Yoga defines this as the science of concentration, of restraining and mastering the agitation of the mind at such a level as to come into complete one-pointed focus within oneself.

The nature of true concentration is not generally understood. I experience this fact every day in my practice. As a somatic healer with a specialty in chronic pain, I frequently see clients who complain of headaches or back tension, and who tell me that these problems come on after they have spent long periods of time "concentrating" at work. The problem, however, is that while they may work hard and produce well according to their own or their employers' standards, they are suffering because they have not learned true concentration.

Concentration is a spiritual art. Like all great spiritual arts, it is profoundly relaxing and centering. People who complain of tension headaches or pain when they do what they call "concentrating" confuse concentration with a certain type of mental and physical strain. This is often a result of having learned to perform on demand during years spent in educational institutions. Because we are judged and graded for our performances in school, most of us learn at an early age to associate performance with anxiety and with generating high levels of internal stress. Anxiety and stress then drive our attempts at focus, and we associate effective work with meeting other people's demands rather than with being absorbed in something that interests us. By the time we grow up, we are so habituated to concentrating in this way that we don't recognize how much tension we bring to our work.

Once we have completed our school years, the competitive and demanding nature of workplace culture encourages more performance anxiety and tension. We learn to exert a huge amount of effort toward directing our attention to the task at hand. We combine focus on a task with stress and nervous tension. Consciously or not, we work in fear, along with the adrenaline rush that we often experience when in fear. While we may be concentrated *on* a task, we are not concentrated *in* ourselves.

True concentration involves a heightened sense of relaxed self-awareness combined with a clear focus on the object of our attention. It is the result not of doing whatever you can to achieve an external goal—the type of behavior often described as concentration—but of learning to control the agitation of the mind and to become tension-free. The more you learn to truly concentrate, the more consistently relaxed, alive, alert and peaceful you feel. Creative geniuses like Einstein and eminent artists like the cellist Pablo Casals knew this instinctively. They accomplished prodigiously, with an endless drive to produce more and more. Their concentration and their work had to be profoundly satisfying, rather than draining, to body, mind and spirit. Genuine concentration is both effortless and tireless.

The primary key to building deep concentration—the inner power that enables you to direct yourself tirelessly and authentically in the world—is to work on integrating deep mental and physical relaxation into any activity. While the following chapters will bring you more fully into the extraordinary art of deep relaxation, you can start making relaxing completely your priority *now*. Then practice approaching your work from that relaxed place, regularly noticing and inhibiting any tendency to tighten up and go into stress.

To integrate concentration with relaxation, begin by observing your breath and by working to breathe in a relaxed, deep manner as you engage in an activity. As this becomes easier, pay attention also to your whole body, and try to release any tensions that you notice in your face and jaw, shoulders, arms, torso, hips and legs. By developing greater body awareness and learning to release habitual tensions, you direct yourself toward effortlessness rather than toward effort. The more effortless you feel, the more your concentration improves.

Imagery can be very effective in learning deeper levels of relaxation. I like to lie on the floor imagining my body melting into the floor and spreading out like a giant puddle. The effect is to release all body tension. If the image of melting doesn't work for you, explore finding another image that invites your body into deeper relaxation.

The more you develop the ability to be physiologically relaxed at will, the more you can integrate relaxation with a specific focus of concentration: listening to someone; cleaning house; working at the computer, and so on. Your goal is to focus on an object or task while maintaining body awareness and relaxation. While learning this takes time and practice, the reward is heightened productivity and pleasure. Develop your practice of learning genuine concentration by exploring the exercise below.

Exercise: Practice concentration

Since skill at concentration builds on the ability to meditate, begin by working enough with meditation to be able to feel and relax into your breathing. Then develop your concentration further by integrating relaxed breath awareness into activity. Start with things that require little concentration, such as chopping vegetables, doing the laundry, or taking a walk.

For an expanded audio version of this exercise, order my MP3 or CD entitled *Breath Awareness* or my *Effortless Practice Package* CD or MP3 at www. ingridbacci.com.

Once you can integrate breath awareness with the performance of simple tasks, add tasks that require greater concentration: writing a memo, presenting a point of view to a colleague, playing an instrument, reading a book, etc. Your goal is to notice when you begin bringing tension into the activity by breathing more rapidly or shallowly, and to make *staying relaxed more important than completing the activity.* Gradually you will improve your ability to perform the activity with greater relaxation. You will also be more efficient.

Step 7: Develop Holistic Awareness and Intuition

Relaxed concentration has a unique quality. It includes a wide field of awareness along with a focus on a specific object, rather like the wide-angle lens on a camera. It is holistic, seeing one thing within the larger context of many interdependent variables. In relaxed concentration you *include* as much as possible in your awareness, even as you focus on something specific. While this may sound unusual, it is an ability that we see and admire in many people. For example, a great tennis player is simultaneously aware of the feel of the ball against his racket, the position and feel of his feet on the court, the distance to the net, the strength of the breeze on his face, and the placement of his opponent. This expanded awareness allows him to take aim with his racket so as to project the tennis ball with precision to a specific location on the opposite court. His skill at placing the ball exactly where he wants is a direct result of his *wide field of awareness*. The more he takes in, in terms both of his own body mechanics, the environment around him, and the movements of his opponent, the more effective he is as a player. It is the player who loses touch with his feet and begins to move heavily, or who is insufficiently sensitive to hit the ball with just the right force, or who fails to estimate the strength of the breeze, who is less likely to place his shot well. He has poorer concentration than his more focused opponent. He fails to practice the holistic awareness of higher level concentration that includes as many variables as possible.

A talented musician, like a talented tennis player, operates with a wide field of awareness. Even while she plays her instrument in her band or orchestra, she can sense the rhythm and tone of her partners' instruments, as well as the atmosphere of the audience. Her ability to play compellingly is a consequence of her skill at taking in and responding to her entire environment. Similarly, a gifted public speaker not only knows his script. He also instinctively feels out his audience as he speaks, senses and responds to its moods and maintains contact with the whole room. His perception is wide-angled, including as much as possible, and his effectiveness comes from this holistic field awareness.

In our linear, left brain world, we often learn to concentrate by *excluding* from our awareness everything except the object of focus. We practice *narrow-point awareness* instead of wide-field awareness. Being totally focused on one thing, we can develop headaches, neck pain, backaches and other pains, both because overly narrow focus tends to create tension, and because, due to our narrow focus, we may not realize that we are tightening our jaw, neck or back in the effort to concentrate. Narrow awareness both shuts down the body and shuts out the environment. For example, we might fail to pick up a relevant suggestion made by a colleague. We can't at the moment let in anything beyond our immediate thoughts, and so we miss out on possibly significant input.

The narrow awareness that characterizes effortful concentration could be likened physiologically to near-point visual work, which converges the eyes and creates tension. The effortless concentration of wide-field awareness could be likened to looking at scenes in the distance, which is known to diverge the eyes and create relaxation. It's when our eyes are relaxed and diverged, not looking at one particular thing, but taking in a whole field that we spontaneously spot that eagle soaring in the sky. If we then point that eagle out to a friend, that friend might have trouble finding the flying bird because he will be searching for something specific rather than relaxing into being open. Relaxed, divergent focus helps us pick up new and often unexpected information that generally comes from unexpected places. To be creative, we have to practice this effortless, holistic concentration.

The way we use our minds dictates what our world becomes. Today, everywhere we go, we can pick up the destructive impact of narrow awareness or overly focused concentration that excludes from consideration things that should not be excluded. Think of the person who is so interested in what he has to say that he can't listen to anyone else. That person is practicing narrow-focus awareness. He is also tense, unpleasant to be with and self-destructive. Life is a lot less fun for him than it could be. Think of the numerous businesses that fail to take into consideration how their operation affects the health of the planet as a whole. They practice narrow-focus awareness on an organizational level. Yet we are all interconnected, we are parts of a whole, we all eventually suffer from the narrow focus that characterizes so much corporate behavior, and our lives can only prosper when we start living from a more wide-angled, holistic perspective.

Think of the medical practitioner who doesn't pause to consider what his patient is eating, or what life problems he is dealing with, both of which could be significant for helping the patient heal. This practitioner is practicing narrow focus. As a result, he may create as many problems for his patient as he tries to solve. I once had a woman come into my office who for the last three years had been prescribed antibiotics for various ailments by her doctor. Even though it is widely known that regular use of antibiotics weakens the immune system, making a person increasingly prone to illness, and even though it is well known that good nutrition is a cornerstone of health, this doctor had never once tried to supplement his antibiotic-dependent approach, and had never asked his patient about her eating habits. By the time she came to my office, her liver (the main detoxifying agent of the body) had become seriously compromised, both because of diet and because of excessive antibiotic use. It took her a year of careful dietary practices to regain reasonable health. This woman had suffered needlessly for a long time because her doctor failed to practice wide-angle vision, focusing too narrowly on short-term drug remedies that can create long-term problems.

The wide-angle, relaxed concentration of holistic field awareness is personally relaxing and creative. It is also socially beneficial. On an organizational level, the more we can be aware of a particular object of concentration or a particular task while including its relationship to everything else in our environment, the more likely we are to be able to act in a way that reaches our goal while avoiding detrimental side effects. Everything in life involves relationships: relationships with nature, with things, with people, and with organizations. Wherever we have relationships, we also have interdependency. Pursuing any goal without full awareness of how our pursuit affects the other relationships of our lives is not just an ignorant practice. It is self-destructive.

Wide-field awareness develops our highest mental capacity: intuition. Intuitive thinking involves a unique mental ability that is inherently gestalt-oriented. It works by *opening the doors of perception* and consistently seeing things in terms of a larger field of awareness, a field that exposes us to phenomena of which we had not been aware until that moment of intuitive insight. When we intuit something, we expand beyond the normal parameters of what we know. We become available to the world beyond our mind. Just as, when we see the eagle in the sky because we were not looking specifically for that bird but were instead simply being open to the sky, so, too, in intuition we become aware of new information because we are not looking for something specific, but instead are just being open to whatever is there. We are practicing field awareness. We release particular ideas in order to perceive and receive.

If we let go of seeing a sibling, husband or friend in the way we have always seen them, we sometimes come to understand them in a whole new way. We see something that has always been there, hidden from view by our habitual constructs. In the same way, if we let go of our habitual ideas about an area—anything from our political views to life after death—we might start to see things in a whole new way.

Intuition develops through the practice of *being receptive*. It is open, taking in as much as possible, without establishing an agenda beforehand. We invite information in rather than seeking to control what we are thinking about. We let go of control in order to receive information from beyond the conscious mind that is stuck in old thoughts. Intuition maintains a friendly and open relationship to the universe. Intuition supports us in developing a loving rather than a fearful attitude toward the world.

Exercise: Develop intuition and holistic field awareness

Intuition is tied to deeper relaxation, which in turn is tied to widening your field of awareness. The following exercise is a classic tool for developing intuition by both relaxing the body and integrating a wider awareness of the body and its surroundings. The result is an empty mind open to new perceptions that can come from anywhere.

An expanded audio version of this exercise can be found at www.ingridbacci.com, as an MP3 entitled *Body Awareness*, or as part of the *Effortless Practice* CD or MP3 package of self-healing and centering exercises.

<u>Lie down in a quiet place and follow your breathing for a few minutes.</u> Once you are relaxed, bring your awareness to your right foot, letting go of any tension you notice. Then expand your awareness to your right foot and calf, again letting go of tension. Continue in this process until you have included your entire right leg in your awareness, up to the pelvis. Then do the same with your left leg. Then become aware of your right and left legs simultaneously. Then continue this process, moving from your pelvis to your abdomen, your abdomen to your chest, your chest to your shoulders, and then down your arms. Then include your neck and head. By the end of the exercise, you will be more present to your entire body. Then, while continuing to breathe in a relaxed manner, include in your awareness not only your entire body, but also the area two feet in front of you, behind you, and to the sides. Finally, include in your awareness your body along with the entire room. You are now optimally present both to your body and to the world around you. This state is the foundation for deeply relaxed concentration and for intuitive insight.

Step 8: Enhance Your Energy

Like everything in the universe, we are made of energy. We function well if our energy flows and poorly if it does not. Deep, conscious relaxation is a tool that allows our energy circuits to open and energy to flow. Once the circuits are open and as long as we maintain the resulting energy flow by continuing to be aware of letting go of passing tensions, we can focus our attention on what we need or want to do, both with a sense of power and from a place of serenity. We optimize our health, our mental focus and our creativity.

To let energy flow through you, you have to clear out the clutter. Executive coaches often teach their clients that in order to find new clients, build new businesses or expand on what they have, they have to clear out what is in the way. They tell people to clean out their closets and desks and to throw away anything that clutters up their space. Professional psychics teach their students the same thing. Clear out the junk if you want to let in what needs to come in. Energy abhors a vacuum and will rush in to fill it. But if you have no space for energy, it won't approach you.

These simple truths can be applied to the way we live our lives on every level. If you want to access your life energy and let it flow, you have to clear out the junk that blocks it. This junk is both mind chatter and physical tension. Clear them out. Make this a priority, rather than the last thing you think of. You think of feeding yourself, dressing yourself, completing your work, going out in the evenings. How much attention do you give to clearing out your mind and body? They are your home. They should be the top priority, not the last priority.

The ancient Raja Yoga science of self-mastery developed an ingenious approach to enhancing concentration and obtaining access to a tremendous energy source. Advanced practices of Raja Yoga teach you how to deepen your powers of focus and relaxed concentration by placing your awareness on various points in the spine or brain that traditionally have been associated with the chakras. These chakras happen to be located at specific central nervous system nerve plexuses. The Raja Yoga practice has a dual effect. It deepens inner calm by taking attention inward, away from the distractions of outer events and mental chatter. In addition, since energy flows where attention goes, the focus on the spine activates the flow of energy through the central nervous system that is the body's energy transmitter.

Ingrid Bacci, Ph.D.

The more you bring your attention into the central nervous system, the more readily energy concentrates into its channel and flows. In Raja Yoga, the process of withdrawing attention from the external environment and into the spine is called *pratyahara*, or withdrawal of the senses. *Pratyahara* develops *total concentration* from a place of *total calm*. At its highest levels, this concentration is focused on the point in the brain at which the electrical circuit formed by the central nervous system connects to the universal source of energy beyond the body. This point, traditionally identified with the *medulla oblongata* of the brain and with the third eye, could be called the transformer point, where energy from beyond the body connects to the circuitry of the body. In Raja Yoga, one achieves states of maximum concentration by integrating deep calm with focusing on this point where the body is charged by its universal storehouse.

Principles of Raja Yoga may seem esoteric and strange to those not familiar with it. Yet Raja Yoga discovered the central nervous system and its importance in regulating all human processes many centuries before scientific inquiry made the same discovery. Raja Yoga's focus on seeing the area of the *medulla oblongata* and brain stem as the critical juncture point for optimizing human function also finds confirmation in independent discoveries made by anatomical science and by Western traditions of body-centered medicine. Some description will clarify this.

The brain sits on the top of the spinal cord. It is divided into four parts by a membrane called the *dura mater*. This membrane also wraps around the entire spinal chord and the interior of the skull. It separates from the skull at certain points to form one sheet of tissue passing through the midline of the brain vertically, and another, horizontal sheet of tissue separating the cerebrum from the cerebellum. The two sheets of this membrane intersect in something resembling a flexible cross at the midpoint of the head, at approximately the physiological equivalent of the third eye, and directly above the *medulla oblongata*. Since this vertically and horizontally intersecting membrane system—in some traditions called the reciprocal tension membrane—is an extension of the protective envelope that wraps around the spinal chord and attaches to the spine, any imbalance of the spine and central nervous system will refer into the membrane system and vice versa. When the body is perfectly balanced from a spinal perspective, the tension between the two membrane sheets of the brain will also be optimally balanced, and the intersection of these two sheets will form a perfect cross in the center of the head, creating the true fulcrum of the body.

Several Western systems of bodywork, including the Alexander Technique, Polarity Therapy, Cranial Osteopathy and Craniosacral Therapy all independently place special emphasis on balancing this physiological fulcrum of the body. Their goal in doing this is to optimize neurological and neuromuscular functioning and to enhance physical and emotional ease. Ancient Eastern disciplines identify this same area as the approximate location of the third eye and the nearby *medulla oblongata*. In other words, the fulcrum whose balance plays a critical role physiologically and mentally in modern Western traditions of healing is located in the approximate area of what Raja Yoga calls the third eye, or sixth chakra. Integrating these different traditions, a balanced fulcrum would be identical with a fully-open third eye. A fully-open third eye is in Raja Yoga identical with maximum intuitive powers of direct perception, with clairvoyance, and with direct knowledge of ultimate realities. It operates as an unobstructed channel to universal energy and consciousness.

Why do various traditions of alternative medicine and the ancient science of Raja Yoga independently converge on an identical place as the true key not only to physical balance but also to optimal mental functioning and transcendent awareness? Optimal physiological balance is identical with optimal physiological ease, and therefore with an optimal state of relaxation or inner tranquility. Since optimal spinal and cranial balance also allow for the easiest flow of nerve impulses through the central nervous system housed in the brain and spinal cord, this will create optimal possibilities of concentration or mental focus. The energy circuit formed by the nerves going up and down the spine will be maximally free to receive and transmit information.

The ancient techniques used by Raja Yoga for full self-realization have a solid foundation in anatomical and physiological therapies that identify the fulcrum of the central nervous system as the key balancing point of the body. Unlike these therapies, however, Raja Yoga discovered this fulcrum in its exploration of *superconscious* as opposed to primarily physical states. In this tradition, profound relaxed concentration on this area—something that can only be achieved as a result of total physiological relaxation and balance—is the key to maximizing energy flow and opening the doors of heightened spiritual awareness and direct contact with the underlying reality of the universe. Superconscious mental states are identical with optimal states of physiological balance and ease.

In Raja Yoga, the ultimate superconscious state of light or bliss is also the state of maximal mental focus, physical peace and energy flow. The more you use tools for developing deep, relaxed concentration, the more you move toward a state that could be called superconscious. Experientially, this integrates profound, expansive inner tranquility with vast energy and ever-expanding intuitive awareness of all that is.

Superconsciousness not only feels good. It is also a much more efficient and accurate guide to living well than the ordinary, limited consciousness of everyday life. In the chapters to come, we will explore in greater practical depth how to build the deepened concentration and access the higher energy centers of consciousness that have been the enduring goal of so many ancient spiritual traditions.

Concentration, as the ancient science of Raja yoga defines it—a state of profound mental clarity combined with profound physical ease—is the answer to all of life's problems. It is the opposite of everyday lack of concentration, the constant involuntary activity of the mind that destroys our sense of physical, mental and emotional peace, compels us obsessively to seek remedy in external transitory experiences, and wears down our internal energy battery. The turbulence of everyday life, with all its restlessness and reactivity, is in complete conflict with the experience of deep concentration that unites you not only with a feeling of profound peace and joy and a massive reservoir of energy, but also with a heightened mental and perceptual capacity. Deep concentration brings with it an unshakeable conviction of being part of something far larger than yourself.

Awareness of a transcendent reality to which we are connected and on which we can rely for information that transcends the ordinary mind is a given in the experience of highly creative thinkers, including some of the most famous scientists, inventors, philosophers and artists in human history. This awareness is also natural to people who devote serious attention to exploring non-ordinary states such as dreaming and hypnotic regression, to psychics and to anyone who spends a great deal of time in imaginal, non-physical dimensions.

From the Raja Yoga and Hindu spiritual perspectives, the recognition of subtler pervasive, non-physical dimensions of reality is a natural result of the systematic practice of the mental disciplines briefly described in this chapter. Hindu philosophy describes the everyday, transitory reality that we live in as *maya*, a world of illusion. This view of transitory reality as illusory is not a hypothesis but a lived experience for those who learn and systematically practice deep powers of relaxed concentration. A great twentieth-century spiritual teacher called Krishnamurti was fond of saying that only when the mind is quiet, free of its own creations, is there a possibility of finding what is real. Genuine concentration detoxifies the mind, allowing it to see and experience what is true.

Modern science tells us that what is real is an undivided field of energy. Concentration is the practice of connecting to that field of energy. Nothing is separate, and all is energy. The ultimate goal of profound relaxation is not only to find an internal state that is deeply at peace; it is also to discover one's own eternity, through the direct experience of being part of an indivisible whole.

Summary

Freeing yourself to live your unique destiny starts with recognizing that your real problems are internal, not external, and that your life will fall increasingly into place when you learn to take charge of your internal landscape. This chapter has traced steps in that process insofar as it applies to the mind. Stages of this process include: recognizing that your inner demon is your mental chatter; beginning to detach from this chatter so as to focus on peace; practicing presence; and applying meditative and concentration techniques that gradually build greater serenity, focus and energy. This process is not only rewarding in itself. It also yields numerous practical benefits and a changed attitude toward life. These form the topic of the next chapter.

4

Finding Your Power through Non-Attachment

It always hurts when you argue with what is.
-Byron Katie, *A Thousand Names for Joy*

Non-attachment is the way to happiness.
-Yogananda, *SRF Lessons*

Cultivating inner peace gives you personal power. It helps you let go of habitual ways of reacting to events, and this opens up your ability to choose. When you enhance your own serenity, your life becomes physically and emotionally healthier as well as more efficient. You also become better at offering a helping hand to those you care for.

Irene woke up nervous. She had had a bad dream. Lying in bed for a few minutes, she let the aftertaste of the dream fade away. She had a big day ahead of her, including a report she needed to complete for a consultancy project. Irene had for the last few years been practicing self-calming techniques, and knew that she would work better if she could stay calm. After a shower and cup of tea, she sat down to meditate. She kept her attention focused on following her breathing, which gradually deepened and slowed. Her mind became quieter. She scanned her body, noticing any signs of tension and releasing them as well as she could. At the end of her meditation she reminded herself that throughout the day she would work on maintaining the inner calm she felt at that moment. She imagined herself going through the day feeling centered and productive. Then she had breakfast and started working.

Things went well until late morning, when Irene's daughter Janice called in tears. Janice's boyfriend at college had broken up with her the previous evening. He wanted to date other women. As Irene listened to the misery in her daughter's voice, she noticed her own chest tightening with anxiety and sympathetic pain. She felt so deeply for her daughter! How could she help Janice in a time of need?

Irene knew that her own anxiety and worry would help no one. Her personal feelings of upset were just variations on fear, and fear only creates negative outcomes. So she listened to her daughter, focusing on calming and releasing her own tensions so that she could be peaceful and resourceful. She didn't offer immediate solutions. She didn't criticize or attack the ex-beau, or say "I told you so." She worked on being non-reactive. She acknowledged how painful the situation was, and after listening and comforting Janice for half an hour, said she would touch base with her daughter again once she had finished work.

Back at the computer, Irene let herself feel the weight of her daughter's sorrow. She realized that although she could feel her daughter's pain, she was relaxed. She let her emotions flow through and then depart. How differently she would have felt just a few years ago! There was a time when she would have become terribly anxious at her daughter's bad news, would have worried in a way that upset her stomach and made it difficult for her to work, and would have been on the phone every two hours to check in on her daughter. Irene smiled. All that frenzy from the old days had really been about herself, not about anyone else. Now she was better able not only to take care of herself but also to be there for her daughter.

Irene finished her report on time. That evening, she had another long conversation with Janice who, on wishing her good-night, said "Mom, I am so happy to have you there for me. You are such a stabilizing presence, and you keep me real. I love you."

Irene had learned the power of inner calm, the calm that comes from making a daily commitment to practicing meditation, deep bodily relaxation, and relaxed concentration. She had tamed many of her own reactive tendencies. She was better at going through life's daily challenges in a way that didn't deplete her, that helped others and that enabled her to be productive. In Buddhist terms, Irene was practicing non-attachment.

Those not familiar with Buddhist thought sometimes interpret the central Buddhist doctrine of non-attachment as advocating not caring, refusing to be involved or committed. This is incorrect. One reason for the misperception of the doctrine of non-attachment has to do with the fact that Westerners often use the term "attachment" to refer to relationships of love. We talk about being attached to people, meaning we care about them. But from a Buddhist perspective, *an attachment is whatever takes you away from inner calm*. Learning non-attachment is learning how to approach life from a place of greater peace. It involves letting go of ego-based needs, or needs based in fear and desire, so as to develop an orientation to life that comes from a quieter, more receptive and open place. Insofar as love relationships involve fear, desire and need, it is true that Buddhism does advocate letting go of such forms of attachment. But it does not advocate letting go of caring.

When you let go of fear-based needs by cultivating non-reactivity, you gain in three ways. You become more peaceful, you become more productive, and you become more caring. Non-attachment in this sense is the ground for all genuine love, and is very different from any attachment involved in relationships of co-dependency.

Non-Attachment Makes for Win-Win

Let's say you have a child who is doing badly in school. You feel frustrated with the child or with his teachers. Practicing non-attachment means that you begin from the assumption that anything you do that does *not* come from inner calm will be destructive to you and most likely harmful to others. While you want the very best for your child, what you focus on dealing with first is your own reactions. If you feel frustrated or upset, you do what you can in the moment to become calmer: not to *appear* calmer, but to actually *be* calmer. You make serenity a priority. Perhaps getting there involves breathing gently for a few minutes before talking to your child or calling the school authorities. Perhaps it involves altering your internal state by imagining yourself in a peaceful environment. Perhaps it involves simply removing yourself from the situation until you are less agitated.

Buddhism recognizes that all agitation is ultimately an expression of feelings of powerlessness and weakness. Learning how to be less agitated is learning how to let go of an inner perception of yourself as in any way weak, deficient or endangered, a perception that makes you reactive.

Once you are able to keep a calm center, you approach situations from a balanced non-reactive place. This makes you a winner. If you are peaceful rather than agitated, you are more likely to be able to help your child or to communicate effectively with school authorities. By being peaceful you are in no way being passive or submissive.

Being peaceful, you are more effective than someone who is agitated. A calm person can communicate strongly, firmly, and effectively, while keeping an open heart and tolerant attitude. No one can listen to someone who comes at them with an axe to grind. Being non-reactive is just plain efficient.

I had a client whose wife suffered for many years from a severe illness. Those years were very stressful for him, and for a long time he stayed up for hours each night, tossing and turning in bed with the anxiety and emotional pain of the situation. While this was an understandable and normal reaction, it doesn't help anyone to react with anxiety and stress to difficult situations. You deal better when you can lessen those reactions, especially since nothing can guarantee that you can avoid having unpleasant or painful situations in your life.

My client with the terminally ill wife eventually developed an ingenious technique for self-calming. When he went to bed at night, he would imagine himself out on a golf course playing the game he loved. To keep his mind from obsessing over his worries, he would start at the first hole and continue through each hole until he fell asleep. In his own way, he was practicing non-attachment, working on letting go of his negative reactions to the painful situation in his life. He slept better and was better able to care for his wife.

Learning non-attachment takes plenty of practice. You have to practice developing a strong foundation in inner peace just as you have to practice playing the piano. If you don't make feeling more peaceful and centered your priority, you are unlikely to recognize that you are dealing with attachment—a need for a specific outcome in a situation—when something makes you angry, upset, or afraid. You are unlikely to recognize that the immediate problem lies in your need and not in the situation. Being attached means being dependent on something or someone responding to you the way you want them to, having your emotional wellbeing focused on something outside yourself rather than inside. Attachments cause unhappiness because they cause people to let external events control their internal state.

Life gives us plenty of opportunity to practice letting go of our reactions of pain, fear, worry, disappointment or rage. I remember one of my first simple learning experiences. Living a fast-paced life, I was on my way home on the highway after a long day of work, and I ran into a massive traffic jam. It was going to take a very long time to get out of this one. I was so irritated! The world, however, was not made to fit into my schedule. I had a choice. I could be irritated, and exhaust my adrenal glands while also ruining my mental state for the next hour, or I could practice letting go of my irritation by focusing on my breathing, relaxing my body, and directing my attention to something useful while dealing with a situation I could not control. I could let go of my negative reaction to the situation. That did not mean looking cool while fuming underneath. It meant practicing feeling peaceful when my personality wanted to feel otherwise. I could make inner peace more important than being annoyed or having to have my way. Every day offers abundant opportunities to develop non-attachment.

Exercise: Practice non-attachment

Make a list of situations in which you tend to feel anxiety, frustration, worry or some other negative emotion. Here are some examples: waking up in the morning with a pile of things on your plate; negotiating traffic jams; sitting at your computer with a deadline in front of you; preparing breakfast for the children before school, while the children are complaining, fighting, or running behind schedule. Once you have made your list, pick one situation to work with when it comes up in your day. Each time it comes up, devote five minutes to experimenting with non-attachment. For example, using your familiarity with breath awareness in meditation, see if you can become more centered and calm in the situation by focusing on following your breathing. Initially, this will take some practice. Keep on focusing on your breathing. Do you notice yourself becoming calmer? Do you become more efficient as well? If so, the situation hasn't changed, but you have. How does this affect others? Are they more responsive to you? Do they become calmer themselves?

Non-Attachment Lets Go of Blame

Let's say you are disappointed with a friend or family member. Perhaps you want your spouse to behave differently: to make more money, or to pay more attention to you. Perhaps your grown-up children aren't meeting your expectations for how they should treat you, for what they should achieve professionally, or for the relationship you expected to have with your grand-children. You are disappointed. If this is the case, then you are attached to someone or something behaving the way you want them to, in order for you to feel all right. If you feel justified in feeling this way, you may experience more disappointment as life goes on, since the chances of others changing to please you are slim.

We often persist in looking at life in a way that gives us reasons to feel disappointed. We may have learned this orientation to life at a very early age. For example, if we experienced disappointment through others at an early age, we may tend to see life as disappointing, and to project disappointment onto our experiences in the future. Just as we have habitual ways of eating, we also have habitual emotional attitudes. One could say a person with a habit of being disappointed is attached to disappointment. Being disappointed fits his comfort zone. We all have emotional patterns that are habits, even though they may seem to be triggered by external events. Most of us have difficulty recognizing our negative emotional habits, because these are embedded in the way we perceive the world. The work of life is the work of shifting out of perceptions that end up causing us pain, into perceptions that bring greater peace and joy.

Wherever attachments exist, negative reactions exist. Non-attachment becomes a force in your life when you recognize that maintaining negative reactions is a dead-end path. That doesn't mean you have to endorse situations you don't like. It just means you learn not to react negatively to them, because reacting takes away your power and your peace.

I have had numerous experiences that gave me opportunities to let go of negative reactions. As an example, a number of years ago, someone whom I had hired as a consultant walked away with the money I had given him without completing the project he had been assigned. I had given him a substantial sum, and I was furious. There was nothing I could do to get the money back, and so I fumed and raged inside. After spending a day doing this, however, I realized that I wasn't accomplishing anything productive by my rage. I was just hurting myself by feeling terrible. I had to let go of my attachment to being treated fairly in this situation, an attachment that made me reactive because being treated fairly just wasn't going to happen. This doesn't mean that I approved of the man's behavior. I just decided not to let his behavior take away my own center. I practiced non-attachment in relation to a small incident.

Letting go of attachments is letting go of depending on having something outside you respond to your needs and desires in the way you want. We act out our attachments most strongly in our intimate relationships. This makes those relationships excellent turf for spiritual growth. To grow is to become both more caring and more independent. The pitfalls of intimate relationships lie in the temptation to be co-dependent.

Co-dependency has infinite variations. It can take the form of compulsively taking care of others, compulsively demanding of others, or any other activity where our own sense of wellbeing depends on how someone else treats us or on how we feel we are treating them. Co-dependency is another word for attachment, because in co-dependency your sense of yourself is tied to how someone else treats you or how you treat them.

When you practice non-attachment, you take full responsibility for your feelings. Whoever or whatever is triggering your negative feelings is not ultimately responsible for them. Their behavior merely highlights your need to change a pattern in your own life. That doesn't mean that you accept situations that are not healthy for you. It means you take responsibility for not continuing in any patterns that invite you to hold on to negative emotions. In one circumstance, non-attachment might require you to let go of staying in a situation that doesn't support your growth. In another, non-attachment might require you to stay in the situation but let go of your own negative reactions. In another, it might require you to let go of your own demands on yourself. The ultimate goal of the practice of non-attachment is to let go of negative emotions. How you do that can vary according to the situation. Relationships function as the stage on which you practice learning what you need to learn and doing what you need to do in order to release yourself from the grip of your own negative emotions.

When I was younger, I once had a boyfriend who was sporadic and unreliable in his affections, and I sometimes found myself thinking of him with resentment. Why wasn't he calling? One day I had a breakthrough. I realized that my resentment wasn't a pleasant feeling, that I would rather not have it, and that I associated this feeling with my boyfriend. I decided I would no longer feel resentment! Initially, I thought of this as taking back my power. I wouldn't allow my boyfriend "make" me feel resentful! Then I realized that regardless of how my boyfriend was behaving, it wasn't he who was making me feel resentful. It was I, myself! My feelings were my issue and my responsibility, not his. Moreover, the most important reason for me not to feel resentful was this: feeling that way made my life unpleasant. No matter how he behaved, it was up to me to figure out how to be free of resentment. That didn't mean I would be his doormat. It meant that I would take responsibility for being happy, rather than giving that responsibility to him. I could now take charge of doing what would be best for me emotionally. Interestingly enough, our relationship quickly changed for the better. We became more independent of each other. We also became better friends. I had let go of using my relationship with this man as a vehicle for feeling resentment, and he let go of using his relationship with me as a way to feel secure by holding power.

I had a client who had a difficult relationship with her son. He was rebellious and angry, and had problems with substance abuse. This mother did everything she could to help her son find a better way. She was deeply concerned for his wellbeing. Yet as so often is the case for mothers, she also needed to feel that he reciprocated the love and support she offered him. Time and time again she would be devastated when he treated her inconsiderately or even cruelly. For any of us, a situation like this would probably be devastating. Yet that is the way things can be if our lives are controlled by our attachments. The lesson this woman had to learn if she was to get out of her own depressions was to let go of needing her son to be the way she wanted him to be. She had to release herself from her own neediness. She had to own her sense of pride in herself, and to understand that, having done the best she could, she also had to let her son be whoever he was. Her life began to improve when she let go.

We are little boats on the big ocean of life. Our rudder is our non-attachment, the ability to keep inner balance and a sense of dignity in the face of life's storms. This takes practice. It also takes realizing that you're not going to rely on the winds of life to take you where you want to go. You will use them where you can, but you'll be able to do just fine even when they aren't behind you. You have your rudder and that rudder helps you navigate from a place of greater stability and enjoyment on life's ocean.

Exercise: Take back your power

Identify a person in your life toward whom you sometimes feel an unpleasant emotion: fear, anxiety, anger, irritation, disappointment, depression, resentment, jealousy, envy, etc. Can you see that you have made that person in some way responsible for how you feel? To help you begin to release your negative feeling, ask yourself the following questions:

a) How unpleasant is this feeling?
b) How long do I want to hold on to it?
c) What would it be like not to have this feeling?
d) How would my relationship with this person change if I let go of this feeling?
e) How am I giving my power to this person by holding on to this feeling?

Finally, imagine what it would be like to talk to this person, or to think of this person, and yet be emotionally neutral. Remember that this doesn't mean that you have changed your perception of the other person; it just means that you no longer react to them the way you did. What happens if you begin to practice noticing and letting go of negative emotions when you think about or relate to this person? Does that person's hold on you begin to dissipate?

Non-Attachment Generates Love

Non-attachment helps you care more. The ability to maintain serenity in any situation is a condition of all genuine caring. The parent who can help the child who is performing badly in school without bringing her own feelings of frustration or upset into the mix is more compassionate and loving than the parent who fusses over or pushes her child. The gentleman I knew who played imaginary golf games in his head to calm himself did not care less for his wife by doing so. He helped himself to function better in giving to her by taking care of himself. The devastation felt by the mother whose son acted cruelly was not a manifestation of her caring for him. It was a manifestation of her need. As she detached more, she was better able to understand the complex patterns of pain behind her son's behavior. She cared not less but more. Her son also treated her with greater courtesy, since his cruelty had in part been a reaction to sensing his mother's insecurity. Her being less needy created an opportunity for him to look more closely at and take responsibility for his own behavior.

You care more and act more effectively when you are less attached, because you are no longer dealing with your ego's need to alleviate feelings of insecurity and craving. You see situations more clearly. How many times have you had a conversation with someone and realized that they weren't hearing you? The person you were talking to was probably attached to his own needs, and interpreting what you were saying through the lens of those needs. He was working from ego instead of from the larger Self, from self-defense instead of from trust. While this behavior is relatively easy to see in others, it is always harder for us to see in ourselves. If you focus your attention on noticing how you feel in your body when you are talking with someone, you will have a good guide to finding out where your ego is. Wherever tension resides, there ego abides. Wherever tranquility resides, from there ego has fled, and you are a clearer lens of perception, more able to absorb what is coming toward you without reaction.

Exercise: Practice not reacting

<u>Observe without attachment</u>. The next time you sit down in a noisy café, at a restaurant, in a train, or even at your own dining room table with your family, take a few minutes to simply follow your breathing, observe the people around you, and notice the conversations. As you do this, be aware of any reactions you might be having. Is the noise too loud? Is someone making a comment you disagree with? Do you like or dislike the way any of the people around you look or act? Notice any negative reactions, and just come back to your breathing. Observe also any tension in yourself, a sure sign that you are reacting. Practice being neutral, curious and peaceful. Do you begin to see the people around you more clearly? Do you understand them better? Can you see how you now have both a more detached and a more loving attitude? You are expressing love by letting people be who they are without reacting.

Non-Attachment Sows Personal Power

A client of mine who suffered from depression had been told she had a biochemical disorder. Yet nothing is purely biochemical. Because we are one whole being, all parts of us participate in creating our symptoms. Whatever was wrong with my client's biochemistry was also a problem in her life. Maggie's ability to care for herself was obscured by emotional attachments that contributed to creating her depression. She began to heal when she took charge of her own feelings by becoming less attached to how others saw her.

Maggie had a habit of taking the overwhelming share of responsibility for the wellbeing of her children and husband. They leaned on her, acted out moods and passive-aggressive behavior patterns, gave her little personal space, and provided minimal emotional sustenance. Maggie was attached to being super responsible; it was her way of proving her self-worth and of being lovable. This made it difficult for her to draw appropriate boundaries and ask family members to take responsibility for their own moods and behaviors. No wonder that she became exhausted, depressed and sometimes explosive.

For Maggie, learning non-attachment was about letting go of having to be there for others at too great a cost to herself. When Maggie established better boundaries, she let go of a habit of feeling burdened. She decided to love her family but not to carry them.

In his beautiful book *Being Peace,* the eminent Vietnamese monk and spiritual teacher Thich Nhat Hanh tells the story of a father and daughter who are performing together in a circus act. One day, the man says to his daughter, "Daughter, we must take good care of each other, because we depend on each other for making a living." The daughter wisely replies, "No, father. I must take good care of myself, and you must take good care of yourself. In that way, we will continue to have a successful circus act." Taking responsibility for your own state of mind while supporting others in doing the same is one aspect of non-attachment.

Exercise: Let go of inappropriate responsibility

Ask yourself where in your life you take excessive responsibility for other people. You will recognize this pattern by the fact that you feel periodically drained, exhausted or resentful. Since many of us learn to care-take others as a way to feel validated ourselves, breaking this pattern can be challenging. What will happen if you stop taking so much responsibility? Are you afraid that you will lose others' affection? Or that the other person or people will make the wrong choices if you stop deciding things for them? Notice that holding on to these perceptions keeps you feeling resentful and judgmental and gives away your power even while you also try to take away power from others. What might it be like to let go of being overly responsible, and to ask others to be responsible for themselves?

Non-Attachment Nourishes Willpower

Imagine you are working on a project that has a deadline. You feel distracted. You want a cup of coffee. Or you're dying to talk to a friend about a conflict you're having with someone. Or you keep on thinking about something that happened last night. Or you can't stop worrying about that toothache you have. Or you feel depressed and want to avoid the project you're working on. Sometimes you give in to these urges and your project lags. At other times, you are able to put aside these impulses and to focus on the task at hand. You exert your will, concentrating on the goal at hand and detaching yourself as best you can from all the thoughts and feelings chasing around inside your head. You practice a small, daily form of non-attachment by not reacting to the random impulses that interfere with moving toward your goal.

Non-attachment enables the development of willpower. Having a strong will is not the same as being willful. Willful people insist on having their own way. It's my way or the highway. Willful people tend to be controlled by their emotions, whereas to have a strong will is to know how to maintain inner balance and calm no matter what, while pursuing your goals. The practice of non-attachment allows you to develop the strongest will possible, letting nothing interfere with your commitment to inner calm and balance.

Non-attachment has nothing to do with being passive in the face of life. The less disturbed your nerves, and the calmer you are, the more capable you are and the better your work is. The world's greatest individuals have been wonderfully calm. Nothing could throw them off balance. A person who becomes angry, distracted, tearful or upset will never accomplish as much as people who have learned to master their reactions, who rarely get angry or lose their center.

Inner calm is a great asset to outer achievement. It takes tremendous self-control to be calm. The mind is like a team of horses chafing at the bit. Letting go of the reins and letting the horses go where they will takes less strength than restraining and controlling those horses. Individuals who can control their own forces rather than being controlled by forces outside them are free.

There is nothing quite as satisfying or as effective as a serene, non-reactive state of mind. A person of calm concentration exerts a cool, determined, steady and smooth-flowing effort of the attention and will toward attaining a definite goal. He is unlikely to be defeated by obstacles, and can consistently work toward goals. Temporary outer defeat does not deter him where it would deter others, and setbacks do not affect his internal equanimity because he does not depend on specific events or time-lines for his sense of personal power. He is a Karma yogi.

One of the ancient sciences of self-liberation, Karma Yoga tells us to work without expectation of reward, giving the fruits of our labors to the Divine. One way to understand this ancient doctrine is that it tells us that the less we depend on garnering specific results from our work, the more effective we will be in working toward our goals.

A person who has made inner tranquility the highest goal cannot be controlled by anything outside and has become free. If each of us could become masters of our own internal states, the world would be a fundamentally different place, free of competition and struggle, yet full of productive, creative energy.

Exercise: Release tension to develop willpower

Identify a project you are involved in. It can be anything from making an elegant meal to running ten miles, to doing a long meditation, to preparing a major report for presentation to the CEO of your company. Pick something that you know challenges your staying power. To see how inner calm nourishes will power, the next time you are engaged in this project, notice when you begin to feel restless. That restlessness will manifest as tension in your body. Refocus yourself by bringing your awareness back to your breathing and seeing if you can identify and let go of the physical tension, whether it is in your neck, shoulders, abdomen, or somewhere else. Do this for a few moments, until the restlessness passes, and then return to the project.

Non-Attachment Attracts Positive Results

Non-attachment is magnetic. When you eliminate your mental and emotional resistance to life's events, you begin to exert a power of attraction toward things that align with your energies. This truth is beautifully expressed in *The Book of Changes*. Also known as the *I Ching, The Book of Changes* is an ancient Chinese text that served as a foundation for the philosophies of both Confucius and Lao-tse. It was developed as a guide to right conduct for Chinese emperors' representatives in the countryside. Centuries ago, such representatives were seen as bearers of divine dictates, and were expected to hold to high spiritual standards of right action. The *I Ching* therefore includes numerous anecdotes describing and advocating wise approaches to various life situations. In one of these, we are told that a man's horse has run away from him. The text counsels us that the wise man does not run after his horse. He knows that if the horse really belongs to him, it will in time come back to him of its own accord. The sage attracts what is right for him.

The wise person
unattached, and you
in its own time. This
really need. People v
ability to be non-gra
resolve your inner c
in the best possible
for specific results,
attachment, or lettin
result. You cultivat
serenity and focus
possible results.

Ingrid Bacci, Ph.D.

speaking event to learn more ab
my speech, rather than worry
over my anxieties and get
from a more detached
to lessen it. Most lik
in the moment. B
day after day
ability to st
Non
of rig
liv

Exercise: Let go of attachment

Is there something that you really want right now? To feel physically better, to get a phone call from some special person, to complete a project that has been hanging over you for a long time? Does it bother you not to be able to get what you want now, or even not to know when or whether you will get it? How might things change if you said to yourself that what you want will come in its own time, if and when it is right for you?

The Daily Practice of Non-Attachment

Non-attachment is a practice to engage in every moment of the day. Practicing non-attachment involves making it your primary goal in situations to observe your reactions and to seek to release yourself from needs, desires and wounds, cultivating calm in place of reactivity. This process never ends. On a day-to-day level, in every moment you can practice letting go of the tension created within yourself by the conflict between how you are reacting to a situation and your ideal of greater inner peace.

Every situation can teach us something about non-attachment. If I am nervous about public speaking, I can use my next scheduled

out non-reactivity. As I prepare for
about the topic or call a friend to talk
reassurance, I can observe the anxiety
lace, and then do what I can in the moment
ely I do not solve my nervousness completely
ut I become a little less compulsive. As I do this
focusing on self-observation and detachment, my
y calm increases.

attachment requires us to let go of the abstract standards
nt and wrong that so many of us try to impose on our
s. What is right in any given situation is whatever reduces
attachment. This will differ for different people, depending on
their attachments and their situation.

A female client came to me with a financial problem. Melissa
and her husband had received a college scholarship for their
daughter, but they were $11,000 short of what they needed for her
education that year. Their house was fully mortgaged, they were
unable to get further financial assistance, and if their daughter
was going to attend college for the rest of the year, there was only
one source of financial assistance that might make that possible:
Melissa's father. Melissa, however, had a complicated relationship
with her father. He had always been emotionally distant, and she
was not comfortable with him. Being wealthy, he periodically
gave his children monetary gifts, but he could also be capricious
in this regard. Melissa felt an aversion to depending on her father
for financial help.

Melissa felt trapped. She had no one else to turn to, but she
was repelled by the idea of asking her father for money. Because
her feeling of repulsion was a negative feeling, it was also an
indication of an attachment. Her attachment to this feeling in her
relationship with her father, therefore, was the problem that she
had to resolve, if she was to become more balanced within herself.
To learn non-attachment, we made it her goal to explore what she
needed to do to let go of her negative feelings.

Our approach to solving Melissa's problem took on a unique
direction. We did not ask ourselves how Melissa should ask for

the money in order to be sure to get it. Even if that accomplished the external goal at hand, it would do so at the price of Melissa's continued aversion to her father. She would have remained emotionally attached. We did not ask if Melissa was responsible in any way for how her father might react to a request. She was not, because each of us bears responsibility for our own reactions, and not for those of others. We also did not decide that she should avoid the whole situation because it was distasteful to her. That response would only have reinforced her attachment, the negative emotional patterns that dominated her relationship with her father.

We focused our primary interest on helping Melissa to use her current dilemma as a vehicle for letting go of her aversion to contact with her father over financial issues. Looking at the decisions she needed to make from this perspective was new for Melissa. She decided she would write a letter to her father making three points: first, her family was in a state of financial need; second, she was making a request of him while fully understanding that he might be unable to meet it; and third, she was perfectly content to accept whatever decision he made. In writing this letter, Melissa worked on asking her father for money from a place of non-reactive neutrality, and on committing herself to being okay with whatever the result was. Once her father responded, she would also get an opportunity to practice more neutrality or non-attachment, no matter what his response.

Our strategy turned the situation into an opportunity for Melissa to free herself from karmic bonds with her father. At the same time that she asked for financial help, something that had always been repellent for her, she worked on asking from a position of neutrality.

As often happens when we practice non-attachment, the results were transformative. Not only did Melissa's father immediately send the money her family needed; he also wrote Melissa a beautiful and affectionate note. He had picked up a change of tone in the way she related to him. He felt closer to her, and he was, thus, able to respond in kind. This had a major impact on Melissa. She realized that her own attitudes toward her father had created some of the negative patterns in their relationship, and that he could be quite a nice man! Melissa had taken responsibility for her own emotional baggage rather than blaming her feelings on her father, and this changed their relationship.

Taking responsibility for your own negative emotional reactions is personally healing at the same time that it tends to create positive external results. My client got the money she needed; she freed herself from her emotional patterns with her father; her father had an opportunity to free himself of his own negative emotional patterns; and a deeper bond developed between father and daughter. The experience laid the groundwork for greater kindness and reciprocity between the two of them in the years to come. When we work on owning responsibility for our own purity of heart, our relationships also tend to become warmer.

Summary

Non-attachment results from an inner practice of making serenity your highest value and then letting the power of serenity translate into effective action in the world. You develop the skills of non-attachment by practicing self-calming techniques, by making your own inner calm more important than achieving specific external results, by letting go of making external situations or people responsible for your feelings, and by slowly developing the strength of will that is the other side of inner calm.

In many ways, non-attachment is about letting go of resistance to allowing life to work through you. Inner peace is nothing more or less than non-resistance. When you no longer resist, you can receive, be supported, and channel energy. When you cultivate inner peace, you automatically take in what you need from the universe, and you give out what is appropriate. You no longer work in a defensive or offensive mode.

5

Healing Your Body's Energy Field

It is through the alignment of my body that I discovered the alignment of my mind, self and intelligence.
-BKS Iyengar, *Light on Life*

In this age of over-specialization, with emphasis on chemistry, bacteriology, and mechanical and surgical research, we have lost sight of the over-all picture of man as a living being with lines of force working in fields of finer energies.
-William Randolph Stone, *Polarity Therapy*

The room was completely quiet. Two dozen people sat in a circle, eyes closed, breathing quietly. I had just finished taking them through a simple body awareness exercise. We had started with the intention of being present and peaceful, letting go of the thoughts in our minds and of the events of the day. Then I had guided everyone through becoming aware of different parts of their bodies, starting with their feet, moving up through the calves, thighs, pelvis, slowly and easily all the way up to the head, paying attention to breathing quietly and deeply as they did so. Periodically, I asked them to notice if their minds were wandering, and to come back to being present to the sensations of their entire body. I reminded them to accept whatever they felt without judgment. We sat like this for a while. At the end of the exercise, each person spent a few minutes writing down what she had experienced during the exercise. Then we were ready to share.

Reactions were individual and unique. Some said the exercise relaxed them physically and mentally. Others said they became aware of tensions they hadn't noticed before. Others said their headache, neck pain or physical tension melted away. Some had sudden, unexpected flashes of intuitive insight. And some commented that they became emotional, or that memories of events they had long forgotten surfaced.

Why does a simple exercise of being present to sensations in your body cause so many different reactions, all of which promote some form of healing, whether by reducing tensions, dissolving pain, releasing buried emotions, or opening up the storehouse of the unconscious creative mind? The answer is simple. *The source of all healing and growth is feeling: feeling without judgment, with pure, total and unconditional acceptance.* Passively feeling the body identifies and releases pain; it identifies and releases emotions; it connects us to our unconscious; and it connects us to insight and inner wisdom.

All feeling comes to us through our bodies. Most of us spend much of our lives avoiding our bodies and living in our minds, in what we think we want to do or have to do. We rarely slow down enough to experience what is going on in our bodies, and we generally do not pay much attention to the moment-by-moment changing flow of sensations inside us. The way we rush around manifests a deep discomfort with our bodily sensations, a desire to control them rather than to be present to them. That discomfort is a discomfort with our very being.

While constant activity and mental chatter can be a way of numbing feelings, it is also true that when we do notice how we feel, we sometimes want to avoid or control what we notice. Enduring and positive change, however, can only happen if we first allow ourselves to experience and accept our feelings for what they are. For many of us, this is extremely difficult. We spend a great deal of time trying to manage how we feel. We think we have to do something about how we feel, or that someone else should. If we're uncomfortable, we try to get away from ourselves, to do something to make our discomfort go away. We judge or suppress how we feel, telling ourselves it's wrong or inconvenient. We spend hours at a time analyzing how we feel, although the resolution of our feelings might come more easily by first letting them surface fully. We argue with, deny or medicate how we feel. We can't just sit with where we are at the moment, and let how we feel work itself through without our interference. To do this may even seem terrifying to some, as though experiencing where we are without trying to control it would be too threatening to endure. In short, we can't be with ourselves. Yet being with ourselves is the foundation not only of real self-transformation in positive directions, but also of the self-love which must begin with self-acceptance. Self-love is in turn the foundation of love for others.

Bodily Presence: The Ultimate Healer

The ability to experience our body's changing sensations without judgment and without reaction is both the road to physical self-awareness and ultimately physical ease, and also the road to emotional awareness and ultimately emotional release and freedom. Experiencing the body is also the pathway to accessing the powerhouse of subconscious memory and creativity, and to mental insight. The simple act of presencing to the body without needing to react frees us, opens us, integrates us, and expands our awareness in all dimensions. While we may need to transform painful physical or emotional sensations, this can only be achieved as a result of first experiencing and accepting them rather than trying to flee or suppress them. By being present to how we feel in our bodies without interference, we stop resisting the flow of life through us. Resisting that flow is the root of physical, emotional and existential pain.

We need to learn just to be with how we feel in order to heal. What, then, are feelings? Physical sensations of all kinds are feelings: a flutter in the gut, an ache in the shoulder, a tension in the leg, an itch on the skin. Emotions are also feelings, and they are most definitely physical sensations. They happen in the body. You can't experience an emotion without feeling it in the body. What are fear, happiness, joy, anger and sadness? They are sensations in your body. We may attach thoughts to such sensations, for example, tell ourselves that we are happy because we are with someone. Yet the feeling of happiness itself is a visceral sensation, and as with all emotions, if the visceral sensation disappeared, so too would the emotion.

Creative insights often come to us as feelings. We feel something is true in our gut, or something just "feels" right, even though we can't say why. Albert Einstein is reputed to have said that his greatest scientific insights came to him as muscular sensations. We also often recognize superconscious states by the fact that they put us in an altered feeling state. We access these states through feelings in our body.

It's the mind that impedes us from being with our feelings. You can't think and feel at the same time. Mental chatter blocks feelings, and since these are the living flow of our energy, mental chatter blocks that energy. Of course, mental chatter is not the only way to avoid being present to our life force. Other techniques include using food, alcohol, drugs, smoking, entertainment, compulsive sex, compulsive shopping, and consumption of all kinds as ways to distract ourselves from being present to how we feel, being present to life as it is living itself through us.

Encouraging you to *avoid* feeling, especially where that feeling can be labeled as "pain" is big business. Whether your pain is emotional or physical, there is a drug to deal with it, and that drug suppresses it. Yet any technique that suppresses sensation is generally counterproductive in the long run, even though it may be soothing in the short term. Let's take the case of physical pain. If we take pills to suppress stomach pain, the aches of arthritis, muscle inflammation, headaches, and so on, this may help us alleviate immediate discomfort, but it also allows us to continue in the habits that created the pain in the first place. We continue to eat the wrong food, not to exercise or to exercise in a way that creates injury, or to drive ourselves into high stress. We maintain our bad habits and medicate the pain away. Ignoring or medicating pain enables us to avoid exploring what may have caused it, and what new habits may serve to release it. Medicating pain keeps us from listening to our feedback system and learning from it, a learning that can transform our lives from being dysfunctional and uncomfortable to being efficient and pleasurable. Medicating pain also encourages us to be passive in the face of pain, to buy into the view that our bodies are beyond our control, and that we are helpless victims of our physiology.

From an evolutionary perspective, physical sensations are valuable messengers. They give us information: about the state of our shoulder or our leg, our abdomen or our lungs. When we are sufficiently attuned to these messengers, they serve a useful purpose, enabling us to maintain maximum health by giving us accurate signals about what is helping us and what is harming us. Pain tells us we need to change something in order to get well, whether that is to eat different foods, to exercise more or differently, to slow down, or to explore how we react to stress. Many great teachers in the healing traditions come to their work as a result of exploring their own pain, whether physical or emotional, learning from it, thereby finding a way to transcend it, and then teaching others how to do the same.

Pain medication is useful under cases of extreme acute pain. Yet these cases are the exception rather than the norm, and usually the result of severe physical trauma. Where severe pain is the result not of physical trauma but of degenerative processes, it is frequently the long term result of ignoring the body's signals or medicating lesser pains, failing to take care of ourselves sooner rather than later. What you ignore eventually turns into a monster.

When you practice being quietly present to your body without an agenda, as in the exercise described at the beginning of this chapter, you often become aware of tensions or pain that you have been ignoring. If you observe these sensations without reaction, they eventually dissipate. This is an example of how pain acts as a messenger that we should listen to. When pain is unconscious as a result of our lack of presence to ourselves, it cannot work its way through the body, and it does damage below the level of conscious awareness. When we stay present to the body, however, painful areas can show themselves and the pain works its way through to resolution. Just as non-judgmental awareness of the breath relaxes the body, so, too, does non-judgmental awareness of sensations, including the sensation of pain. When you have pain of which you are conscious, simply being present to it with interest and curiosity can in many cases help it to dissipate. What you don't resist won't persist.

Just as physical pain is a messenger, so, too, is emotional pain. Just as we block physical pain in the search to dull experiences of discomfort, so too we block emotional feelings that involve discomfort or conflict. We do this in two ways. First, we refuse to *slow down enough* to fully experience where we are. We keep on the move, and if we keep on the move frequently enough and for long enough, the feelings that we react to by keeping on the move simply get buried. Second, we *try to control uncomfortable feelings* rather than sitting with and learning from them. We may take medication to suppress our anxiety or depression, something which leaves the cause of those feelings unaddressed. We may eat or drink or smoke. We may seek the stimulation of conversation or exercise to get away from feelings of discomfort. And we may act out our feelings through efforts at manipulation and control, whether of ourselves or of others. Yet all of these approaches end up suppressing a part of ourselves, removing us from our authentic feelings, and creating a dumping ground of unprocessed unconscious feelings that build inner turbulence. Ultimately, that inner turbulence is simply an expression of our lack of love for ourselves, our judgmental and harsh relationship to our own inner dynamics, and our inability to practice gentleness toward the experience of ourselves.

In the body-presencing exercise described at the beginning of this chapter, some individuals reported that emotions came up for them, and some reported flashbacks to emotional situations from their past. These emotions came up spontaneously as a simple result of feeling their bodies. When feelings come up in this way, they come up because they need to be acknowledged, processed and resolved. They have been ignored, only partially acknowledged, or suppressed. The practice of being present to the body automatically helps a person process these emotions, leaving that person somehow changed.

Being present to emotions through the body helps people let go of blockages to their growth. They don't do it by thinking about their emotions, analyzing their emotions or talking about their emotions. They do it as a result of being present to their bodily sensations, which allows them to feel previously unrecognized emotions, emotions that express the truth of where they are.

Being present to your feelings has nothing to do with being "emotional." So-called emotional people tend to be reactive and conflicted, rather than comfortable with themselves. They have difficulty containing and processing how they feel, and instead act out reactions to those feelings on the world around them. Someone who is "emotional," who argues readily, gets hurt or upset easily, or drinks or smokes when unhappy is someone who can't contain and process her emotions. She can't let the waves in the ocean of life wash through her, trusting that her little boat will ride those waves safely. She can't find the peace that comes from learning to be at peace with the rising and falling tides of emotional life.

The word "emotion" comes from the Latin word meaning "to move out of." Emotions in themselves are neither good nor bad. They are waves in the flow of life. When we can accept and feel them fully, rather than react to them and try to take control of them, they move through us, bringing joy or sadness, heat or cool, fear or anger, and then they fall away, just like the waves of the ocean. If we sit with them, they bring wisdom in their train: the wisdom of knowing and acknowledging what is in the depths of our hearts; the wisdom of reaching resolution of emotional experiences as opposed to conflict and suppression; the wisdom of knowing that no emotion needs to cripple or dominate us; and the knowledge that underneath waves of emotion is deep peace. We can experience those waves and still stand. We are our emotions, but we are also something enduring and profound beneath those emotions.

It is the emotions that are blocked, judged, incompletely digested, repressed or controlled that become negative, chronic and explosive. Anger, frustration and fear are all normal everyday emotions. When we sit with them as we experience them viscerally and without reacting to them by trying either to control them, or to control something or someone outside ourselves, they either dissipate on their own, or reveal to us what it is we need to do next in order to continue to be balanced. It is only when we try to manage emotions by controlling ourselves or others that these emotions become chronic and toxic. We end up in a war with ourselves. Inevitably, when we are at war with ourselves, we will also be at war with others.

Because presencing non-judgmentally to the sensations of the body is ultimately relaxing, it provides an extraordinary tool for accessing intuition, insight and creative vision. Thomas Edison developed many of his own inventions by practicing deep physiological relaxation as a vehicle for "hearing" innovative ideas. Most of us are familiar with experiences where we just "feel" that we have to go in a certain direction, and we recognize later that we were right even though we cannot explain logically why we made the choice we did. The body's sensations, if we are willing to listen to them, act as a powerful source of intuition and effective guidance.

The Synchrony of Mind, Body and Emotions

Practicing presence to your body, while taming your tendencies to react to and control what you feel, reveals an essential truth known by ancient sages but often buried by the fragmented and overly specialized approaches of contemporary science and culture. *How you feel mentally, how you feel physically, and how you feel emotionally are all reflections of a single fact: how present you are to your body.* The more present you are to your body, the calmer your mind will be, the more peaceful your emotions will be, and the more released physically you will be. Similarly, the less present you are to your body, the more agitated your mind will be, the more turbulent your emotions will be, and the more physically tense you will be.

Your mental, emotional and physical states are completely interdependent, and they are varying manifestations of an underlying reality: the relative tranquility or turbulence of your body and of the energy flowing through you. There is a *synchrony* of mind, body and emotions that tells you that healing one heals the others, because they all heal through the same process of *being present non-judgmentally to your body and to the stillness that underlies and supports your energy flow.*

The synchrony of mind, body and emotions as interdependent expressions of your degree of bodily presence and tranquility implies that when you are in an optimal mental state, you will necessarily be in an optimal physical and emotional state. When your mind is quiet, you are physically relaxed, your emotions are also peaceful and you are present to your body. Similarly, when your mind is turbulent, you are physically tense and emotionally agitated, and you lack non-judgmental presence to your body.

Just as mental balance necessarily correlates with emotional and physical balance, so too emotional balance correlates with mental and physical balance. When you are in an optimal emotional state, you will necessarily also be in an optimal mental and physical state. Finally, when you are in an optimal physical state, you will necessarily also be in an optimal mental and emotional state.

This synchronistic relationship of the different dimensions of your experience can be charted as an equation of mental, emotional and physical states, where the physical state includes both muscular levels of ease or contraction and patterns of breathing. In an optimal state of being, where you are fully present to your body, this equation of different states looks as follows.

Chart I

**Deep muscle relaxation and quiet, easy breathing
= Calm focused mind
= Peaceful, expansive and joyful emotions**

Just as there is a synchrony of mind, physical body and emotions in your optimal state, so too there is a synchrony of these three in your sub-optimal states. When your mind is distracted, overactive or insufficiently focused, your body is necessarily in a state of excess tension, your breathing is restricted, and you feel negative emotions ranging from tension or anxiety to anger. Similarly, when your breathing is restricted, or your muscles tight, you necessarily suffer from emotional and mental tension as well. And when you feel negative emotions, your mind necessarily tends toward agitation, you are physically tight, and your breathing is restricted. This equation of mental, physical and emotional states in a sub-optimal condition can be charted as follows:

Chart II

**Muscle tension and restricted, shallow breathing
= Unquiet, poorly focused mind
= Negative emotions of fear, anger, depression, impatience, etc.**

The synchrony of mental, physical and emotional states has a number of important implications for your personal journey into full self-empowerment:

1. Because your state of mind is precisely linked with a specific physical and emotional state, and a specific physical state is precisely linked with specific mental and emotional patterns, you can't improve any single one of these without improving the others. If you want to maximize your mental state, you have to optimize your emotional and physical states. If you want to optimize your emotional state, you cannot do

so without also optimizing your physical and mental states. You can't ignore any one of these while trying to improve another. Rather, your best route to achieving optimal functioning and self-actualization is to choose a path that works with all of these simultaneously. For example, if you are working hard at the computer and get headaches or back pain, or feel tense in the chest, improving your mental function will require you to relax physically and release underlying anxiety or frustration. In a similar vein, any deep physical healing necessarily includes healing on a mental and emotional level. And in the same way, deep emotional healing inevitably has a profound effect on your vitality and ability to focus clearly.

2. Because all healing and self-empowerment ultimately depend on your ability to be quietly and non-judgmentally present to your body, the high road to full healing and self-empowerment lies in becoming present by *discovering, exploring, mastering and releasing all tensions in your body*. Full bodily aliveness, achieved by being completely present to your body, by virtue of allowing for full bodily relaxation also results in full emotional balance and mental focus. In fact, practicing bodily presence is the surest and most effective route to emotional and mental balance.

3. The body is the container for the energy flow of your life. Whenever you experience mental, emotional or physical tension, you suffer from *restricted and distorted life energy*. You are directly aware of this when you feel physical tension. Restricted energy also has a unique signature in your mental and emotional experience. For example, when your mind is unfocused, it carries static or noise, like a poor radio transmitter. That is an inefficient energy flow that tends to be accompanied by physical tension. A person

with mental static is energetically jammed. Similarly, stressful emotions feel like a form of disturbance or turbulence that disrupts the smooth flow of both feeling and thought. These are all variations on the theme *of inefficient, distorted, blocked, disrupted and chaotic energy flow.*

4. Life-affirming physical, emotional and mental states all involve *expansive and fluid* expressions of life energy. These are the automatic result of practicing deep presence to your body, since presence to the body is an act of acceptance, and acceptance allows for flow. The more quietly and non-judgmentally present you are to your body, the more it feels soft, open, relaxed and radiant. Because you are fully present to yourself, your circuits function easily, and you flow out into the world easily as well. Your mind is calm and quiet, so that you quickly assimilate information, just as the clear channel of a radio transmitter quickly picks up and responds to signals over a long distance. Your emotions are fluid and non-turbulent. You rapidly resolve and release negative emotions, and are left with a basic feeling of joy and peace, an openness of being, and a lack of restriction. You feel physically both profoundly relaxed, sensuously alive, and deeply energetic. This aliveness means that you shine brightly and widely, like a radiant star, rather than glimmering, sputtering or dying out altogether. When at your very best and most self-actualized, your energy state could also be likened to an open sky, a smoothly rushing river, or a calm lake. Interference is minimal.

You are free when your energy flows easily. You learn to experience your energy and to let it expand and flow in and through you by connecting to your body. Meditation helps jumpstart this process by connecting you to your breath, slowing and deepening your breathing, and beginning to calm your mind. Other body-centered tools further refine this process, showing you how to feel and release subtle tensions throughout your body, to open up more deeply and to move from energetic and physical contraction into expansion and liberation. By learning to feel how you block energy, whether physically or emotionally, you are able to let go of the blockages and eventually to expand out into a larger energy field. You train yourself to notice and then change certain habits. You let go of restrictions you have unconsciously built up against experiencing the full flow of life.

In the course of a lifetime, we all respond to many situations by tightening up in self-protection. Over time that tightening can cause chronic tensions and pain as well as mental and emotional restrictions. As you develop the ability to be present to yourself, you become more aware of and are able to release physiologically based contractions.

If you've ever been in a car accident, you know that you can become very tentative in your driving until the memory of the accident fades and your natural confidence returns. Most of us are not so lucky in all our experiences. We clench and recoil over the years, building one defense after another against the not-fully-digested blows of fate. After a while, we become one giant knot of restrictions. To become free is to undo your knots. You learn how to let go of your knots one at a time by experiencing how you are inside without trying to defend, and then gradually rediscovering yourself in a body that is lighter and less defended. You learn how to soften. The softer you become, the more undefended you are, and yet the more powerful. You are strong because you no longer need to defend.

Steps to Healing

There are many stages in the process of greater presencing into undefended aliveness and power. The first step in the process is conscious physiological relaxation.

Step 1: Feel the Softness of Your Body

Release begins with being present to yourself and accepting how you are and where you are in your life. Acceptance is the single most important step, repeated again and again throughout a lifetime, in the journey of self-healing. This piece is crucial because ultimately, all tension is based on self-hatred, on the failure to accept yourself. You are perfect because you are meant to be who and where you are. This does not mean that you should not change, but rather that change begins with full ownership of your love for yourself, and love sees whatever is as perfect, even as it transforms it through the power of acceptance. What is loved can release and change precisely because it is loved.

We all tend to be addicted to trying to do something about ourselves whenever we are uncomfortable. Yet experiencing discomfort without reacting to it is the key to healing. Your body automatically lets go of tensions and sensations that you accept. Allow your tension to be there and observe it. Just as a person will often stop arguing with you if you simply listen, so, too, body tensions will gradually dissipate if you simply observe them. Spend time each day being present to your sensations. Don't think about them, live them. Feel every inch of your body with curiosity and without judgment. It is who you are right now, in the now. Everything else is just mental construct. See if you can enter into the dance of simply feeling yourself in this moment, without thought, with simple, straightforward appreciation of the depth and range of physical sensations happening in you. This process, repeated again and again, begins to teach you not only how to relax, but also how to find the enduring stillness and peace that lies underneath relaxation.

While non-judgmental awareness of sensations helps release any tension or pain, you can further encourage this process through *imagining*, as you feel your body, that it is becoming *softer*. This encourages physical release, since softness is the experiential correlate of relaxation. The softer your body feels, the fewer restrictions you have, the more physical pleasure you feel, and the calmer you become.

Imagining softness enables you to sidestep the chronic habits of your body and mind, and to go directly to a deeper layer of healing. Images work where thoughts cannot; they help you find greater softness because they don't engage you in trying to do something. They generate their effects on a non-doing, subconscious level. When you imagine softening, you give your brain a tool that it can use to help your body release more deeply than it knows how to do on a conscious level. One of my favorite images consists of picturing the breath as a gentle wave caressing me on the inside. I also like to imagine that my body is as soft as a baby's or that it is a strand of seaweed floating on ocean waves.

As an example of how the image of softness can help release physiological tension, I recently worked with a friend suffering from an acute attack of back pain. The muscles of his low back were in intense spasm, and he had been to the chiropractor several times without significant relief. When we worked together, and while I was manually encouraging his tissues to release, I also asked him to imagine the tissues of his pelvic area softening and relaxing, and to breathe into them. As he did this, he experienced significant relief.

While personal practice is the foundation of learning deep body release and softening into your core, certain forms of bodywork can offer useful support. Craniosacral therapy, a subtle form of hands-on therapy aimed at releasing deep body tensions, is profoundly relaxing, can access unconscious bodily tensions, and introduces clients to states of physiological ease that they may never have experienced before. Once clients are aware of these states, they can move toward them more easily on their own.

Being soft isn't about being flaccid. It's about being alive, open, vibrant and confident. Great athletes have a palpable softness and grace to their movements that are lacking in the more driven, rather rigid qualities of less accomplished competitors. Babies are very soft, yet they are extraordinarily strong for their size, and very alive. They move easily, flexibly and tirelessly. To become fully ourselves we need to relearn the soft, vibrant aliveness of infancy. This is intensely pleasurable. It teaches us the true meaning of self-love. To love yourself is to be comfortable in your own skin, with no sense of tension or confinement, to be soft.

The powerful aliveness of bodily softness is the goal of breath awareness techniques that form an integral part of Buddhist teachings, as well as many of the martial arts. When you can let your breath be infinitely soft, your boundaries melt and you have no fear. You can accomplish some of this simply by imagining your breath as soft, then softer, and then even softer.

If you explore breathing your way to softness, remember that there are no right and wrong, correct and incorrect ways to breathe. There is only softness, a natural and inevitable result of letting go of having to make your breathing happen in the "right" way. If you use a particular breathing technique, use it with awareness that breath work is about learning how to use your own feedback to let go of tension. If a technique helps you let go of tension, adopt it. If it does not, let it go. Find what invites you into softness. Don't be seduced by some notion of correct technique that misses taking you to your real goal.

Stephen Levine is a well-known author and healer who spent many years practicing presence to the processes of dying people. He found that to be really present to dying people, joining them rather than trying to do something to or for them, he had to become soft. He experienced this as combining vulnerability and strength. He further explored both the beauty and the power of softness on an odyssey of the spirit that he shared with his wife. In *Embracing the Beloved*, he recounts how the two of them lived for a year in a mountainous area where they maintained complete solitude and silence. Without words or company other than each other's physical presence, they discovered an extraordinary intimacy and depth. Levine repeatedly uses the image of "soft belly breathing" to describe how he experienced this opening. Day after day, as he and his wife explored simply being together, without additional frills, tasks or agendas, they found their breath opening, softening, and pulling them into exquisite depths of feeling. They reached into the core of their mutual aliveness.

An ancient Zen proverb tells us that only when we can be extremely soft and flexible can we be extremely hard and strong. Why is it that people like the Dalai Lama and the Vietnamese monk Thich Nhat Hanh earn our enduring admiration when our respect for others might fade? Their softness is not only appealing in a harsh world, it is also the other face of their indomitable will and clarity of purpose. Whatever is soft and yielding is as powerful as water, and water, as we know, can wear away stone.

Softening is the foundation for higher levels of performance. Great musicians attain their preeminence by cultivating an extraordinary delicacy and softness of touch. Some of the martial arts train advanced practitioners to achieve higher levels of performance not by doing more but by doing less: by using less force and greater subtlety to achieve goals that force cannot achieve. This contrasts strongly with that part of our gym culture that emphasizes strengthening and working isolated parts of our body, often without reference either to the amount of work expended in the effort, or to the efficiency of movement involved, or to integration of the body with the mind and spirit. The results of gym routines are thus sometimes only muscle deep. Building muscle mass and working out on treadmills have value for cardiovascular health and strength, but they do next to nothing for organ health, flexibility, and emotional and mental attitude. These require subtler arts that emphasize body awareness and mental presence as key elements of health.

Practicing bodily softness makes you more receptive. A brilliant violinist is receptive, having infinitely soft hands that respond to and allow the notes to flow through him; a good listener is receptive, opening to allow others to share their deepest thoughts; a creative thinker is receptive, opening willingly to the power of her subconscious; a great healer is receptive, with hands that are exquisitely attuned to the needs of her client's body.

Moshe Feldenkrais was an extraordinary twentieth century somatic healer and innovator who helped thousands of people both to improve physically and to address mental and emotional challenges simply by having them explore how to make various movements more softly, with less and less effort. He recognized that chronic pain and mental and emotional distress both manifest as bodily tensions, and that reducing those tensions can often address physical, mental and emotional issues more effectively than taking a pill, undergoing surgery, or seeking psychotherapy. Feldenkrais knew that softness is non-resistance combined with an opening to energy and to the unknown, and that physical hardness promotes mental and emotional rigidity, insecurity and judgmentalism.

In the process of his explorations, Feldenkrais also discovered what a powerful tool for bodily transformation the use of visualization could be. He frequently showed his clients the releasing power of visualizing softness and effortlessness through the following type of exercise. He would have clients work directly with mobilizing and freeing up tensions on one side of the body. Then he would have them do the same thing *in their imaginations alone* on the other side of the body. Astonishingly, the side that was treated only in imagination generally ended up being freer than the side that had been mobilized and treated through movement!

Feldenkrais was one of the first modern somatic explorers to found his work on the intimate connection between physical tension and emotional insecurity. For this reason, he utilized exercises and visualizations that released physical tension as important tools for personal growth. Feldenkrais also knew that the intrinsic connectedness of physical, mental and emotional tensions had deep implications for an approach to healing, and he recognized the importance to our health of mastering our inner dynamics. For example, he reasoned that if we did not cultivate our ability to be present to our bodies and maintain a state that is both relaxed and energized, the massive stresses of living in a fast-paced world would inevitably put us in chronic tension and stress, both of which could, in turn, lead directly to chronic pain. Feldenkrais was right.

It's no wonder that modern society is experiencing an epidemic of hip and knee replacements, not to speak of back surgeries and of the increasing incidence of treatments for arthritis even in the young. The constant compression and contraction of the musculature that people experience through daily stress squeezes down on their connective tissue and bones, eventually causing bones and cartilage to deteriorate and arthritic deposits to develop. A daily practice of consciously letting go of bodily tension can therefore help one avoid pain and surgery, improve physical health and flexibility, and contribute to a sense of increased confidence and vitality.

Mental, physical and emotional fitness all develop through consciously integrating softness into movement. This benefits the organs, is physically rejuvenating, and promotes mental and emotional balance. The softer the body field, the more space internal organs have to function freely, the more easily fluids flow through the body, and the more easily nutrients reach their destination while at the same time toxins are released. On many levels health is identical with flow. Learning to soften is the subjective corollary of learning to open to greater internal flow.

Exercises: Feel and soften

1. Take five to ten minutes each day to feel and soften into your body. You can do this at the end of an exercise session, when you wake up in the morning, at bedtime, or some other time of your choosing. Lie down quietly and let your body sink into the floor. Take enough time so that your mind gradually becomes quiet and your body feels more relaxed. Then gently focus your awareness on one part of your body. It can be your face, your chest, your abdomen, a hip or leg, whatever appeals to you. Take time to explore the sensation of this area. Let yourself be interested in feeling the smallest of sensations. As you begin to feel more and more, your body will become softer and more alive. Then imagine that the part of your body that you have chosen to focus on is becoming even softer,

melting away any subtle tensions. As you do this, you might also like to move this part of your body very gently and fluidly. How can you minimize the effort and maximize the fluidity of this body part? What does it feel like to focus on gentle movement aiming continually for less tension and more softness? What does this tell you about how much tension your body holds habitually?

2. <u>When you lie in bed at night, spend a few minutes before you go to sleep letting your body melt into the sheets.</u> Feel the support of the bed underneath you. Let go completely. Dissolve into the sensation of letting go. Make this your evening ritual, a delicious way to release the restrictions of the day. When you awaken in the morning, rather than jumping up, lie there and imagine being completely relaxed in a pleasant setting. Absorb the feeling of that image into your tissues. Get out of bed continuing to visualize that your body is completely relaxed. Begin your day this way. You are inviting change deep into your core.

3. <u>Explore moving with minimal effort.</u> Try performing some simple activity, for example walking, typing at the computer, rolling on the floor, with minimal bodily effort and maximum feeling and softness. In walking, how does your walking change if you pay attention to really feeling the sensation of your feet, and to feeling fluid and soft in your feet? What happens if you get into feeling the movement of your hips? Do you start to walk differently? Do you enjoy your sensations more? Do you notice and can you let go of any stiffness? In typing at the computer, what changes if you focus on allowing your face or your hands to be really soft? In rolling on the floor or exercising, what happens if you focus on some part of your body, exploring how fluid, soft and alive it can feel while you are moving?

For audio exercises exploring moving with minimal effort, see my *Inner Flow* exercise in the MP3 or CD series *Effortless Practice,* and my *Reduce Your Chronic Pain* DVD, at www.ingridbacci.com.

4. Consider sessions in craniosacral therapy to help you let go of restrictions deep in the body, and to experience profound relaxation. Look for experienced practitioners in your area by going to www.iahp.com, or contact me directly for recommendations or for craniosacral therapy sessions, at www.ingridbacci. com.

5. Consider some lessons in Feldenkrais Awareness through Movement. For information on practitioners in your area, go to www.feldenkrais.com.

Step 2: Move from Softening to Expansion

Getting more connected to your body can have interesting and unexpected consequences. Every experience of releasing physical tension has two consequences. On the one hand, you experience greater physical ease and aliveness. On the other hand, because you are more in touch with your body and more sensitive to it, you also become more aware of subtle layers of tension and holding of which you had previously been unaware. You become simultaneously aware of how free you can be—much freer than you ever might have imagined—and of how profoundly contracted and constricted you have been, a shell of neuromuscular and neurological defenses wrapped up in the illusory protection provided by ego, that part of us that needs to compete, to compare, to prove and to defend itself.

This dual awareness has dual consequences. First, you recognize that at each level of your journey into yourself, you can continue to find the next layer of release and softness, through the use of imagery, non-judgmental body sensation, and similar techniques. Second, you realize that you can also combine softening with more proactive techniques to free yourself. You can gently but firmly *dig* to gain access to age-old contractions. You realize that learning to expand into your full self, rather than contract into your shell, is going to involve a dynamic, active process side by side with a gently passive, receptive one. It is therefore time to learn how to dynamically expand out of your shell, reaching into and transforming deep layers of hidden tension and contraction.

If you look at an amoeba under a microscope after it has been poked, you see that this simple, one-celled organism immediately contracts in self-defense into a tiny space. It seeks to isolate itself as much as possible from what it perceives as a hostile environment. Give it some time, however, and it gradually begins to spread out to its original size. Given more time along with a welcoming environment, and it will continue to expand outward.

We, and all animals, are in certain respects very much like amoebas. When we feel ourselves to be in danger, we contract. We need to relearn the natural state of health, a state of expansion, of reaching out triumphantly in all directions. What is this like? Think of antelopes or cheetahs in the wild. They stand beautifully tall, their bodies reaching up to the heavens. When they run, their limbs reach out fully in all directions. Think of the spread of wings of birds in flight, and of their heads and tails stretching out in front and behind. Think of a tree growing unobstructed, its roots reaching deep into the earth, while its branches also reach up and out, gloriously seeking to expand further and further. We love the expansiveness of nature. It reflects the fundamental impulse common to all living things. We are maximally healthy and alive when our limbs and torso expand triumphantly in all directions, giving us plenty of internal space and expressing our joy in flowing out into the world.

Much as animals in captivity often lose the grace of their wild counterparts, we have forgotten how to expand into our true state of grace, empowerment and flow. Feeling and softening into ourselves through simple awareness and imagination prepares us for the next step—learning the art of expansion. Expansion involves actively stretching muscles out in all directions, challenging age-old contractions just enough so that they can begin to soften further. Dynamic expansion is both liberating and strengthening. It's learning how to become as big as we are, how to stretch out and own our space. It's learning how to become kings and queens, princes and princesses. To learn this natural state of grace and power, which is as much an emotional and mental state as it is a physical one, we need to turn to physical disciplines that actively teach us how to expand.

Two preeminent disciplines teach the art of expanding into your full energetic space, so as to own physical, mental and emotional effortless ease, fluidity, grace and strength. They are the Alexander Technique and the branch of Yoga that teaches postures called *asanas*, and that has traditionally been called Hatha Yoga (Not to be narrowly identified with the specific *asana* Yoga training program that has adopted the term Hatha Yoga as its brand name.). These two approaches teach you how to reduce the effort you exert in any given movement or posture, while at the same time utilizing principles of expansion to stretch and open up the body at increasingly deep levels. To access this expansion, both of them also invite you to become deeply familiar with bodily sensation, bringing heightened awareness to patterns of tension and release that ordinarily remain unconscious. Of the two, the Alexander Technique tends to stress conscious mental mastery of physiological sensations, while Yoga *asana* practice tends to stress achieving greater awareness and mastery of physiological sensations through dynamic movement.

The Alexander Technique

The Alexander Technique, best known as a tool for reducing back pain and enhancing grace, poise and flow, was first developed by Frederick Matthias Alexander in the late nineteenth and early twentieth century, as a method for improving breathing and voice control. Over time, it developed into an educational instrument that could be utilized to improve all levels of physical, mental and emotional function. Today, the Alexander Technique is most widely taught as a method both for reducing neuromuscular and skeletal pain and for improving the performance of many artists, especially actors, musicians and dancers. The Alexander Technique is widely taught in many of the world's premier institutes for the performing arts.

Frederick Mathias Alexander based his work on a simple recognition: *whenever you focus your primary attention on what you want to accomplish rather than on how you are in the moment, you tend to bring tension into your body.* This tension starts with a tightening in the back of the neck, which in turn triggers further tension down the entire length of the torso. As Alexander was fond of pointing out, physical tension makes you mentally, physically and emotionally less efficient at achieving your objective. It is therefore counterproductive to place your primary attention on achieving your objective. Instead, you should focus on eliminating any physical tension that might be triggered in the attempt to attain the objective in question, so as truly to function both more efficiently and fluently. When you place your primary attention not on what you are doing but rather on releasing the tension in your body as you do whatever you are doing, you tend to improve on all levels. You feel more at ease, you focus better, and your performance improves. Alexander described and taught the process of releasing bodily contractions as a widening and lengthening of the entire body—in short, as an expansion.

Alexander realized that our all-too-human emphasis on achieving "results" actually subverts our ability to be present to what we are doing, induces contraction, and therefore results in impoverished performance. With this insight he went on to develop a systematic approach to teaching people how to become aware of and release the subliminal tensions that cause them to underperform, to become anxious, and eventually to become ill or to develop chronic pain. The essential elements of this approach were twofold: learning to pause and inhibit the automatic tendency to tighten when engaging in any performance; and then replacing this automatic tendency with conscious direction to release and lengthen the neck, and release, lengthen and widen the torso and limbs.

Alexander used his hands as a gentle teaching tool, touching parts of the body and bringing awareness to these parts, while also integrating verbal suggestions with his touch. As he worked, he always began by helping his students recognize and inhibit habitual tension patterns, particularly in the head/neck relationship, an area whose muscle contractions play a primary role in triggering tension throughout the rest of the body. From the head and neck, he would also include awareness of the entire torso, suggesting that the torso could move out of its contractions by lengthening and widening. His work enabled students to consciously lengthen their entire spines and widen their entire torsos, effectively going from contraction to expansion.

Despite its unorthodox nature, Alexander's work became widely known, and people as eminent as authors Aldous Huxley and George Bernard Shaw, as well as the illustrious American philosopher John Dewey, credited him with dramatically improving the quality of their lives. Famous scientists of the time, including Raymond Dart and the neurophysiologist Charles Sherrington, viewed his work as extremely significant scientifically. Ethologist Nikolaas Tinbergen devoted much of his Nobel Prize acceptance speech in 1973 to a description of the benefits of the Alexander Technique, claiming that it offered invaluable body-centered tools for improving the quality of life on all levels. He concluded:

> I can do no more than characterize, and recommend, the Alexander treatment as an extremely sophisticated form of rehabilitation, or rather of re-deployment, of the entire muscular equipment, and through that of many other organs. Compared with this, many types of physiotherapy which are now in general use look surprisingly crude and restricted in their effect—and sometimes even harmful to the rest of the body.[4]

---

4   Nikolaas Tinbergen, Nobel Prize in Medicine Acceptance Speech, December 12, 1973.

Today, the Alexander Technique is widely taught in England, Ireland, Israel, and parts of continental Europe, where the culture tends to embrace preventive and educational approaches to health and healing. It is taught to a lesser extent in the United States. Alexander Technique teachers use techniques based on Alexander's core insights and teaching methods. For example, a teacher might instruct you, while you sit, stand or walk, to notice, inhibit and release any tension in the neck, and to imagine lengthening and widening through your torso. Simultaneously, the teacher might touch your body in a way that invites heightened awareness of the area in question, helps you release tension, and contributes to lengthening and widening. Over time, you learn how to consciously use mental processes combined with body awareness to reduce tension, to expand, and to find greater lightness of being. Used consistently, Alexander Technique principles can have a profound impact on mental, emotional and somatic processes, and can contribute to dramatic improvements in health. All these effects also turn you into a different person: lighter, happier, more at ease with yourself and with the world, and more able to manage difficult situations and emotions as they arise, without defensive posturing.

As you work with softening and releasing tension in your own body, the Alexander Technique can provide you with tools to identify more clearly where tension exists and how to release it. The process of release is mental, achieved through conscious mental direction and imagery, along with subtle somatic hands-on guidance from a teacher. Because it connects you so profoundly to your body, and heightens your awareness of how to use mental direction to release tensions, the Alexander Technique is an ideal companion to Yoga *asana* practices that use more dynamic, active stretching to achieve greater flow. The Alexander Technique will, in fact, contribute to an increased ability to use Yoga postures to achieve the inner quietness, expansiveness and sense of freedom that are the ultimate goals of Yoga.

Yoga Asanas

Yoga *asana* teachings are similar to the Alexander Technique insofar as they are based on the ancient philosophical, psychological and somatic system of Yoga, called Raja Yoga, that recognizes that all mental and emotional stress, and most disease, has an origin in somatic contraction. Like the Alexander Technique, Yoga *asana* classes focus on teaching expansiveness—the ability to open and reach out in all directions, freeing the body from years of contraction and defense. Unlike the Alexander Technique, most Yoga classes are fairly dynamically energetic and proactive. This dynamism can have both positive and negative consequences. On the one hand, many people in Western culture engage in Yoga mostly as a form of athletic exercise, and fail to use the body awareness and self-reflection that can make the practice of *asanas* not only a physically strengthening experience but also a profoundly transformative process that creates inner quietness and deep levels of peace. On the other hand, if Yoga *asanas* are approached as a tool for studying the mind-body connection and becoming more centered, and if you approach them as a vehicle for learning softness, flow and stillness, they can be radically transformative. In fact, the dynamic, strenuous and challenging aspect of Yoga, if approached with an understanding of its ultimate goal of softening and effortless expansion, can provide opportunities to reach deep into the body that may be missing from the softer, more receptive and mental approach of the Alexander Technique. The blend of dynamism and inner awareness that uses that dynamism to achieve tranquility corresponds to the true goal of Yoga *asana* practice which, as an integral aspect of the larger practice of Raja Yoga, is to find self-liberation.

Yoga practices take students through postures or *asanas* that open and stretch the body maximally in all directions: for example, reaching up to the sky all the way through the fingertips while reaching down into the earth all the way through the heels, balls of the feet and toes; or lengthening the torso to the fullest extent, while reaching with arms and legs in opposite directions. Each posture asks you to expand in opposing directions, using that process of expansion to identify deep areas of contraction, and to coax those areas into releasing and opening. Postures can be strenuous, as they challenge students to free up joints and activate muscles that have lain dormant or remained tight for years or even for an entire lifetime. The challenge of these exercises is to find a way to simultaneously lengthen, strengthen and balance all the muscles of the body. The end result is a radiant expansion outward from the spinal core of our being at the navel. Ultimately, this training results in an extraordinary combination of feelings of ease, grace and power, a strength and confidence that move us outward into the world with no need for self-defense, rather than inward in an attempt to protect and defend.

Obtaining the full mental, emotional and physical benefit of Yoga *asana* practices requires not only time and commitment, but also deep attention to the internal experiences of the postures, so as to release any observed tensions and open the body, develop awareness of the emotional and mental correlates of those tensions, and build an increasing sense of physical ease along with greater mental clarity, emotional balance and inner quiet. Yoga is an extraordinary tool for finding mental, emotional and physical peace combined with power. Since learning this involves self-observation and fine attention to detail, as well as deep physical change, it is best to start Yoga practice by working with traditions that emphasize this combination. One of the best systems to study in this regard is Iyengar Yoga. Founded by B.K.S. Iyengar, this system of Yoga emphasizes precise instruction and long holding of poses. While to the casual observer it may look less dynamic than many forms of Yoga, it is also more likely to create deeper, more positive and lasting change than classes that look more superficially athletic. Yin Yoga, an approach to *asana* training developed by Paul Grilley, involves long holding of specific postures so as to stretch deep into the connective tissue, and is also useful.

Once the principles of Iyengar Yoga are grasped, and once regular practice of Yin Yoga has rendered deeper tensions in the body more accessible, other more dynamic approaches to Yoga such as Ashtanga or Vinyasa systems can provide further inroads into the expansive opening to spirit, freedom and ease offered by the practice of Yoga *asanas*. It should be kept in mind, however, that Yoga classes unfortunately are often taught with too great an emphasis on speed. For learning inner quiet and deepening release, it is critical that a Yoga student be able to quiet his mind in each pose, holding it long enough to find greater balance, poise, and stillness.

Of all the books written on Yoga, Erich Schiffmann's book *Yoga: The Spirit and Practice of Moving into Stillness* most clearly captures the process of Yoga *asana* practice as a discipline that combines infinite softness and self-awareness with dynamic strength and flow. It is a "must read" for anyone who wants to move beyond the athleticism of many contemporary Yoga practices and into the possibility of using that ancient discipline as a tool for self-liberation.

If you are interested in finding your way to optimal ease in your body, you might try combining a movement therapy like the Alexander Technique, which heightens your daily body awareness, with regular practice of a Yoga discipline that retrains your connective tissue into its optimal state of flexibility. If you have chronic physical issues, you might also get further assistance and guidance by working with a skilled craniosacral therapist who can help to release deep unconscious tensions from your body, and speed you on your way.

The ancient founder of Yoga philosophy and practice, Patanjali, and the founder of the Alexander Technique, Frederick Mathias Alexander, both knew that there is no such thing as a thought or an emotion that does not have its corollary expression in a physiological state. They also recognized that any thought or emotion that is related to tension or compression in the body is necessarily self-destructive, and that this tension is related on some level, subtle or not so subtle, to fear. Today, both Yoga and the Alexander Technique are widely known as tools for building greater physical flexibility and ease, and for resolving chronic pain. Yet the deeper value of these disciplines is that through teaching profound presence along with expansion of the body, they enable students to live in their bodies, hearts and minds as powerfully centered, open and calm individuals. They are less affected by the currents of life because they have trained their systems to live at full throttle and at the same time with a big heart. We would all do well to embrace this type of deep healing that moves us into radiant aliveness in our own bodies.

Exercises: Integrate softening with expansion

1. Explore the Alexander Technique so as to develop your ability to release tension and expand into your personal space. Find a local practitioner, or research where to get more information and locate practitioners, by going to www.alexandertech.org in the United States, www.alexander.ie in Ireland, or www.ati-net.com for other countries. Alternatively, visit www.ingridbacci.com for workshops featuring movement awareness to expand your sense of self and to release tensions.

2. Explore Iyengar Yoga. Whether or not you already practice Yoga, your understanding of the discipline will deepen by working with a skilled Iyengar Yoga teacher in your area. You can learn more by going to www.iyengar-yoga.com and by reading books by B.K.S. Iyengar, the founder of this system. Alternatively, visit www.ingridbacci.com to find out about workshops that include Iyengar Yoga practices as part of total self-healing and empowerment.

3. To deepen your flexibility and release ingrained tensions, explore Yin Yoga , the approach developed by Paul Grilley, and described through his DVDs and his book *Yin Yoga* .

4. To find support on your inner journey, and to develop a deepened understanding of how to use Yoga postures as tools for self-liberation, read Erich Schiffmann's

Yoga: The Spirit and Practice of Moving into Stillness.

Step 3: Open the Perceptual Field of Your Body

You can live contracted—physically tight, mentally tense and emotionally closed down—and you can live expansively—physically relaxed, mentally balanced and emotionally unafraid and at peace. How you live depends in part on the nature of your perceptual field which, like your body, can be closed or open, contracted or expansive. If you change the way you perceive, expanding beyond your habitual field of perception, you will change the way you feel and live.

Susan came to me complaining of neck and shoulder pain. I guided her through a simple exercise to help her feel all aspects of her body in a more integrated way. We built her awareness step by step, starting with having her absorb the space occupied by her feet, then including her feet and her calves, then her feet, calves, and thighs, then her feet, calves, thighs and pelvis, and so on, all the way up to the crown of her head. At the end, though I had done no hands-on bodywork with Susan, her pain was gone.

Susan's pain reflected the fact that she did not occupy her whole body with her perception. Her awareness of herself was confined to her neck and shoulders. The more she hurt, the more she focused on these areas, and the less she felt the rest of her. She was not aware that as her attention narrowed in focus, her tension increased, and that she worsened her pain by focusing on it. This was not purely for psychological reasons. The pain was real enough, a reflection of the fact that a narrow focus of attention goes along with bodily tension, and a broad focus of attention goes along with relaxation and ease. When Susan became present to her whole body, to a wider field of awareness than was her norm, the shift in her focus enabled her to release pain. How we feel physically and emotionally is affected by how narrow or inclusive our field of perception is.

Energy flows where attention goes. If you practice continually integrating all of yourself into your awareness—your feet, legs, torso, arms, hands, neck, and head—you automatically improve your mobility, sense of ease and balance, physical health, emotional peace and mental calm. If you have pain, anxiety or mental tension, you almost certainly have unconsciously narrowed the field of your awareness. A narrow perceptual field contracts your energy.

Being present to your whole body makes you more expansive, energetic and released. Being present to the space around you as well can further contribute to these positive outcomes. I was teaching a class in Alabama, and one of the participants excused herself to go to the bathroom. When she came back and headed toward her seat, her whole body said, "Let me make myself small." She contracted energetically and physically as a way of making herself less visible and apologizing for what she thought was interrupting the class. Somewhere she had learned that being a good person required her to take up less space, but the space she diminished was the space of her own energy field.

I asked her to go out of the room and then to come back in. This time, as she entered the room she was to feel that she owned it, that she had an infinite amount of space. As she walked in, she held her head high and her body looked relaxed, arms swinging gently by her sides. Now she looked both soft and confident. The entire room around her relaxed. The quality of her energy was infectious.

We took a moment to break from the class curriculum, have everyone walk around the room, passing by each other in close quarters while imagining that they had plenty of personal space around them. People loved it. They realized they had spent their lives making themselves small. An energetic exercise like this teaches you how to use your self-awareness and presence in space to feel secure and expansive, like the bright star of energy that you naturally are.

Owning a lot of space has nothing to do with how much physical room you take up or with how much attention you require. The more expansive you are inside yourself, the less attention you need from others. You simply feel well. When I was a teenager traveling the chaotic New York City subway system and feeling terrified of life, I felt very small and afraid. I had no personal space. My inner smallness attracted negative behavior from others, and people often picked on me or jostled me, consciously or unconsciously recognizing me as easy prey. Now I can travel the subway system, sit in the most crowded of conditions, and feel like I have infinite space. My energy remains expansive, and I end up having wonderful conversations with unusual people. Expansive personal energy invites expansive energy in return.

We live under an illusion that sees the "other" as a danger to ourselves. This is the basis of energetic and perceptual contraction. If you live in fear of others, there is no way you can live without contraction. To expand your own energy field is to let go of fear and to see the world as one with you.

A good start to balancing and expanding your perceptual and energy fields is to become more consistently present to your whole body, whether by practicing self-awareness techniques on your own or exploring movement therapies like the Alexander Technique, Feldenkrais Awareness through Movement, Yoga, Tai Chi and Qi Gong. As you practice being present to your body, see if you can release any tensions of which you become aware. Then take a minute to close your eyes, and with your eyes closed, become aware of the space a foot in front of you. Include it in your awareness of self. It is your space, your energy field. Let yourself own it. Then expand your awareness to include a foot behind you, and then a foot to the right and to the left. Notice if it is harder to expand in one direction than in others. This will indicate to you that your energy field is restricted in that area. Keep on expanding in all directions, to fill an area as wide and deep as the room, and then beyond, including several miles in either direction. The more space you occupy energetically, the more relaxed you are and the more in touch with your energy field. Do this first as a meditation, then practice owning a wide energy field as your daily reality. When you are in a restaurant eating with friends, include the entire room in your awareness. On a walk outside, see your personal space expanding in all directions as far as you can imagine.

When I first began exploring exercises such as the ones just described, I thought they were interesting New Age gimmicks and did not give them much credence. Now I know better. Exercises in perceptual expansion are excellent tools for feeling more at home in the universe and for discovering and releasing our own subtle forms of resistance. They also help develop high sense perception, telepathic capacities, and connection to our spiritual source. You are a miniature radio transmitter. When you expand your awareness, you begin to develop the ability to reach beyond your body and to see, hear and feel beyond the immediate environment. Because you are vibrational in nature, an electromagnetic field within a larger electromagnetic field, your intelligence is not limited in space and time. I relearn this every day in my practice as a medical psychic. Years ago I learned how to access information about someone's physical, mental and emotional state while knowing nothing more about them than their name, age and gender. This ability is a direct consequence of having learned to expand my perceptual field and to attune myself to subtle vibrations. You can do the same.

Exercises in perceptual expansion are tools for breaking the illusion of separateness. The more you expand your awareness, the more connected you feel to the universe around you, until you recognize that you *are* the universe and it *is* you. Enlightenment is the lived experience of this truth, along with all the freedom that recognizing this truth brings.

Exercises: Expand your perceptual field

1. Practice being present to your whole body: your feet, legs, pelvis, torso, arms, neck and head. This is especially important if you have chronic pain issues and if you tend to spend a lot of time in your head. Practicing being present to your whole body will reduce both mental static and pain. For further

support, download the MP3 *Feeling Your Body* from my website, www.ingridbacci.com. This exercise is also included as part of the package, *Effortless Practice*, available either as a CD set or as MP3s.

2. Practice integrating whole body awareness into your daily activities. Use this to notice more readily when you are becoming tense, and to release your tension more quickly than you might otherwise do.

3. Integrate body awareness into daily life. When at work, whether it be at the computer, performing another task, or dealing with people, see if you can integrate body awareness with being aware of the room around you while you are also aware of the task at hand. Your expanded awareness will reduce the effort involved in whatever you are doing.

4. Imagine your own energy space spreading out beyond the confines of your body. Practice walking around with an expansive feel. Notice how comfortable this makes you, and how you can integrate having lots of space for yourself with giving lots of space to others.

Implications of Our Vibrational Reality

You are not matter. You are energy. Your body is the congealed, denser expression of the energy field that underlies it. Individual parts of the body—limbs, organs and other tissues—are only particular manifestations of this field. Each individual body part is what it is and functions the way it does as a result of its relationship to the whole body and to the body's electromagnetic field. Individual organs, muscles and other tissues do not exist separately from one another. They exist as wrinkles in the web of the body's field, just as the body is itself a wrinkle in the electromagnetic field of the larger universe. Traditional medicine has yet to fully grasp that mechanical and biochemical treatments of physical problems artificially isolate one part of the body from the whole on which it depends. You always have to address the whole body in treating any local issue. Full healing also requires that you treat the whole body in its relationship to the mind and the emotions.

Gifted hands-on healers work holistically to address problems in a given area of the body as expressions of whole body distortions, and these whole body distortions in turn as expressions of imbalances in the underlying energy field. The energy field is a holographic whole. When healers work with repatterning the energy field, they work holographically, giving the body information that allows it to re-set itself in a more functional pattern. In this way they are able to enhance the health of the whole body while at the same time resolving a particular presenting symptom. Holistic healing reaches to the very core of a client's issues. If the vibrational template of the body remains distorted, no amount of tissue work on specific areas will correct it permanently, since all parts of the body are interrelated, and since the body patterns itself according to its underlying template. Corrections that do not address the vibrational template or ideal balance of the body lose their efficacy over time. The old problem resurfaces or a new symptom emerges.

Summary

Each part of the body is what it is through its relationship to other parts of the body, and the body as a whole is what it is through its relationship to mental and emotional patterns, and vice versa. Mental habits find their reflection in physiological patterns, and emotions live in and express themselves through the body. The profound interconnectedness of all aspects of ourselves has, in turn, further significant consequences. By working directly with bodily awareness and presence, you can not only free up your body and expand your energy; you can also achieve ever-deepening mental focus and calm, and ever increasing emotional serenity and heartfulness. Techniques to expand bodily self-awareness include whole body relaxation exercises, physiological softening,

Feldenkrais work, the Alexander Technique, Yoga practices, Tai Chi and Qi Gong, and playful exploration of perceptual expansion. Learning to live in the body from a place of physiological freedom is learning to live from a place of mental clarity and emotional authenticity as well.

The place of physiological freedom is a place of ever increasing softening and expansion. We live in our bodies, and our bodies are by nature dense relative to our spirits. Yet the more aware we become of our bodies, and the more present we become to them, the more this body becomes a spiritual experience: an experience of lightness, softness and depth. The more we encounter that lightness, softness and depth, the more we feel ourselves to be unbounded, a part of the universe rather than separate from it, and the more we flow with the current of life.

There are, however, times when accessing our inner selves challenges us to release deep emotional holdings, holdings that ultimately reflect a distrust of ourselves, a refusal to know who we really are, and therefore sometimes even a punitive relationship to ourselves. Meeting those parts of ourselves involves the journey of emotional healing that forms the subject of the next chapter.

6

Healing Your Emotional Body

Ninety percent of pain is emotional. Imagination is our worst enemy. There is a spasm in the emotional field before the spasm in the spine and body.
-William Randolph Stone, *Health Building*

A new client was on the phone. Emily had called to say she had cancer for the third time and she wanted to set up an appointment. She had treated her first bout of cancer through chemotherapy and radiation. When the cancer returned, she had healed through extensive nutritional work. Now the cancer was back again, and she felt there must be something that she wasn't addressing. We made an appointment for the next day.

Before Emily's appointment, I sat down to meditate and use my medical intuitive skills to see what I might pick up that could be of use. When the information on Emily came through, it did so in a familiar way, with a peculiar sensation that I have learned to respect. That sensation feels like a laser beam hitting its target, or a satellite docking in at a station. There is a subtle click in my mind followed by an image. In Emily's case, the image was so strange that I was taken aback. I was looking at vicious tentacles gripping the right side of Emily's chest. I wasn't sure what this meant, but Emily certainly looked to me like she was under attack from a very dark force. I made a note of what I had seen and prepared for our session.

When Emily arrived, she told me that the cancer was in her ovaries. There seemed to be no relationship between her presenting symptoms and what I had seen. Yet experience told me that the connection would reveal itself.

Emily wanted to explore whether bodywork might help her address the recurring cancer. She lay down on my bodywork table and I scanned her body with my hands. As I did this, I felt a powerful blockage in her right chest, in the same area where I had earlier seen the tentacles. Gently putting my hands over this area, I invited Emily's conscious and subconscious awareness to join me there. Startled, Emily told me that her first bout of cancer had occurred in exactly that area, in her right breast. We were quiet for a while, as she and I connected more deeply to her body's hidden wisdom.

Energetically-based hands-on therapy can sometimes stimulate and reawaken emotions and memories held in the tissues. Buried emotions like these need to be relived so as to be cleared from the body. If not, they can contribute to pain and disease. It came as no surprise to me that Emily soon began processing some painful experiences.

As an infant and a young child, Emily had been sexually abused by her father. He would hold her down forcibly, pressing on her chest—where her cancer eventually appeared—when he abused her. The tentacles I had seen in Emily's chest were certainly an appropriate image for her unconscious emotional memory of this terrible trauma, a memory that was now coming to the fore. Repression of the traumatic memory had possibly contributed to the growth of the cancer.

Incidents from the past flooded into Emily's mind, along with all the disgust, repulsion, rage and hurt that she had been unable to express, first as an infant and later as a child. Experiencing these difficult feelings was both overwhelming and cathartic. My job was to support Emily in finding the courage to relive what she had tucked away from conscious memory and hidden in her tissues. Emily realized this was important, sensed it might somehow help her heal, and went home determined to continue processing the painful feelings until our next session.

When Emily came to my office a week later, she unbuttoned her blouse and showed me that her entire chest had broken out in an angry, puss-filled rash. I found this extraordinary. Emily's emotional release of toxic, repressed emotions had triggered visible physical detoxification! This was the most dramatic direct evidence of the connection between repressed trauma and disease that I had ever witnessed. To me, it demonstrated unequivocally how internalized trauma and unexpressed rage—both the result of the abuse—can foster chronic illness.

As Emily and I continued to work together, emotional detoxification was regularly followed by physical detoxification. The rewards were well worth the effort. At the end of six weeks, her oncologist told Emily she was free of cancer. She was also free of the suppressed emotional garbage of pain, fear, disgust and hatred that had resulted from many years of terrible abuse. It has now been a number of years since I initially worked with Emily. In the intervening time, I have seen her on an occasional basis, and her cancer has not returned.

Suppressed Emotions and Disease

Unacknowledged emotions, feelings that are too overwhelming or painful to experience at a given time, become blocked bodily energy. This is why suppressed negative emotions play a powerful role in the etiology of disease. If you do not find a way to accept, experience and release emotions, if you have to block them, they remain submerged in the form of tissue memory. This energy block depletes your life force and provides a breeding ground for illness. The blocked emotions continue to control you because instead of being expressed and then dissipating, they fester unresolved and unexpressed. You continue to be dominated by and live in the unresolved past, even when you are not consciously aware of this fact.

Emily had suppressed her feelings of terror, disgust and betrayal because when she experienced them as a child, there was nothing she could do to defend herself. She had unconsciously decided not to feel because to do so was too painful. That means that she also held on to her feelings subconsciously, unwittingly creating the toxic breeding ground for her disease.

Blocked emotions turn against their owner. When we refuse for whatever reason to feel our feelings, we reject them, and that means we reject ourselves. When we reject ourselves we create a divided camp within. When Emily had learned to avoid feeling her anger, pain and rage toward her father, she had also learned to hate who she was. She unconsciously interpreted the fact that she had to deny her own feelings of anger and rage as meaning that those feelings were wrong. They were bad, and therefore she was bad. As so many children do before they earn sufficient independence to think through situations for themselves, Emily had long ago taken responsibility for what was wrong in her world. She had subconsciously interpreted experiencing something terrible as meaning that there was something terribly wrong with her. Emily's life story is one that many of us repeat in our own way. Our suppressed emotions typically find their companions in self-blame and self-hatred. Consciously or unconsciously, we feel inadequate and wrong.

When we repress our feelings, we lock ourselves into a position of feeling and acting disempowered. We identify with being a victim. We see the world outside us as bigger and more controlling than we are. We live in blame. We may blame ourselves and we may blame others. Most likely we do both. When we heal, we let go of blaming ourselves and blaming others by recognizing, processing and releasing the suppressed feelings that have led us to adopt a victim stance in the world.

The forces of self-hatred and self-denial can make it difficult for us to contact the feelings we suppress. This is a primary reason illness develops. No one wants to be ill. Yet illness can be a call to action, because it sometimes signals that an inner problem is not being addressed. Crises like serious illnesses can play a significant role in challenging us to confront our inner demons and to empower ourselves. Finding the story under an illness can help us recognize buried pain and unacknowledged feelings, and this can enable us to resolve the patterns of self-victimization that result from holding on to a past that remains frozen in our subconscious and in our bodies. Discovering, reliving and releasing our story yields greater self-acceptance, self-love, improved health and greater resiliency.

The Healing Power of Bodywork

Because the body is the storehouse of the subconscious, and repressed memories are held in tissue contractions, bodywork is essential to full healing. You can approach some of this healing work through meditative and breathing techniques if you are able to stay with feelings as they rise to consciousness, and to let them be what they are. You can also use movement modalities such as the Alexander Technique and Yoga, which free up bodily restrictions, to help the subconscious rise to the surface. For many of us, however, the taboos around repressed emotions, and the loneliness associated with our repressions, are so great that we need the gentle witness and skilled guidance of bodyworkers trained in the art of emotional release. Hands-on healing work such as craniosacral therapy can provide extraordinary assistance in liberating the unconscious emotions buried in the body. This has been the case for me, as well as for hundreds of clients who have sought my assistance.

A client named Janet came to me complaining of chronic pain which for many years had not been successfully treated. When I worked with her, I felt an enormous amount of compression in her head, and I brought my hands gently to that area. She was quiet during most of the session, but at the end reported to me that she had had the strangest experience. It felt to her as though she was being born, and was having trouble moving through the birth canal! She had the impression of being in tremendous pain, and of nonverbally asking her mother as she was struggling through the canal, "Why are you making it so hard?"

Janet had entered an altered state. She had never had an experience like this before, and she wondered whether she was fantasizing something about her birth. My reply to her was first to ask her how she felt now that the session was over. This is always the most important variable in evaluating altered state experiences. She reported experiencing a sense of both release and relief. I told her that this was a significant sign of healing, and that it suggested that whether or not her altered state experience corresponded to actual facts, it held an emotional truth for her that she needed to process. I also suggested that she ask her mother about her own memories of giving birth to Janet, in case that confirmed that Janet might have been re-experiencing her birth.

In his seminal work, *The Holotropic Mind*, Stanislas Grof records the results of thousands of interviews of individuals who had intrauterine and birthing experiences under hypnotic regression or under the influence of psychedelics. It is now widely recognized that memories of our entire lives, including experiences in the womb and at birth, remain in the subconscious mind. In craniosacral therapy it is fairly common for clients to regress to events around their birth, and I did not doubt that Janet's altered state had been related to actual experiences. She needed to confirm this for herself, however. When she returned for her next session a week later, she told me that her mother had confirmed that labor had been long and difficult, and that the doctor had ended up using forceps to deliver baby Janet. Janet was amazed that her experience on the table reflected actual events. As for me, I had found an explanation for why Janet's head was compressed and severely torqued on her spine. The combination of continuous pressure as she came through the birth canal, and the application of forceps to the still-forming, soft bones of her head, had created enduring compression of both the head and neck. The type of compression Janet suffered generally goes undetected by doctors unfamiliar with craniosacral therapy, but it can create numerous complications, whether immediately or over time as a result of increasing strains put on an infant's body as it grows toward adulthood. The physical trauma Janet had experienced in coming through the birth canal had generated lifelong repercussions in her chronic experiences of struggle and pain. If she had had the opportunity to have craniosacral therapy as an infant, the compression and trauma could possibly have been repaired, and Janet's life would have been fundamentally improved.

When early physical trauma such as Janet experienced is a contributing cause of later symptoms, I work together with my client to help release both the physical compression and the accompanying trauma of the original experience. Physical trauma that has a strong emotional cathexis will not leave the body unless the emotional imprint of that trauma is also released. As Janet and I continued to work, she had more birthing experiences as well as early childhood memories that circled around feelings of being unwanted by a mother who was busy with younger children. What her mother had actually felt and intended in the relationship with her daughter was not relevant to Janet's physical and emotional healing at this time. What was relevant was for her to be able to acknowledge and experience what childhood had been like for her, independently of her parents' intentions.

The physical constrictions in Janet that resulted from the birth process had given her a poor start, making every stage of development more physically challenging for her than it might have been. The emotional isolation she experienced compounded that problem. As she gradually unraveled her story, Janet realized that because her early life had been so physically and emotionally difficult, she had unconsciously interpreted this as meaning that there was something wrong with her. She had learned to survive by constantly pushing herself, never asking for help, and always seeking to please. No one else paid attention to how she felt, so why should she? Her own difficulty in caring for herself, learned early and as a result of necessity, led to her being emotionally harsh with herself, which in turn created tension that stressed a body that was already under-functioning and in pain.

As Janet heals, she not only continues to remember elements of her trauma and to acknowledge the tremendous pain and loneliness she experienced as a child. She also learns to make love of self as important as taking care of others. She learns to recognize that her internal monologue is often self-punishing, and she works to replace this monologue with kindness and compassion. Such kindness to oneself is difficult to learn. It has nothing to do with taking vacations, buying nice clothes, or getting attention from others. To show compassion toward yourself is to still compulsive internal voices of self-criticism, anger and fear, and replace them with nurturing acceptance, understanding and care. For most of us, the journey of changing our internal monologue from one of self-criticism to one of compassion, support and inspiration takes years of regular practice.

Compassion for ourselves has many faces. Sometimes it requires simply taking time to be alone with our own thoughts and feelings. At other times, it means allowing ourselves to be more vulnerable with others, to share what we have never shared because it's important to trust the feelings of our own heart, even if that is scary. At other times, compassion toward ourselves requires us to put up strong boundaries against others' demands, to own our own space with others in ways we may never have done before. On a daily basis, compassion for ourselves requires that we cultivate inner tranquility as a more important asset than any outer accomplishment. And of course, compassion for ourselves can also help us find the courage to risk pursuing a vision of our unique life path that is deeply meaningful to us, no matter what the odds, and no matter what the opinions of those around us.

No one outside you knows better than you what your life's solutions are or what your purpose is. These are uniquely yours to discover and to experience. They emerge as a natural outcome of letting go of all forms of self-victimization. Teachers and mentors on the path of life can be useful, but you know for sure that you are on the right path for yourself when you feel strong enough to own that you no longer need such authority figures in your own life. The great spiritual teacher Krishnamurti was fond of saying that no church, no doctrine, no philosophical study, no specialist, and no guru will ever give you the answer to your life's questions. You alone have the answers to your questions.

Exercise: Explore the emotions hidden in your pain

If you suffer from chronic physical pain or illness, consider seeking assistance in resolving possible underlying emotional and spiritual issues that are contributing to your problem. Work with a body-centered therapist who can help you access the emotions concealed in your body. Your best choice will be someone who has extensive experience in craniosacral therapy and who is skilled in integrating emotional release work into sessions. You can contact me at www.ingridbacci.com, or you can look up craniosacral therapy on the Internet or go to www. iahp.com for a listing of practitioners in your area.

Self-Hatred and Guilt: The Ultimate Foes

In his wonderful book, *The Disappearance of the Universe*, Gary Renard writes "People may *think* they want to be free, but they're really not willing to give up their own way of looking at things."[5] Nowhere is this more true than when it comes to feelings of self-hatred and guilt. The greatest psychological challenge each of us faces is the challenge to let go of our negative emotions toward ourselves. That's where ultimate healing lies.

My client Emily who healed her cancer discovered that she had a voice inside her head that continually said, "I hate you, I hate you." She belittled herself every moment of every day. This voice was the introjected voice of her father, who used those words in abusing her. Part of Emily's healing lay in recognizing that this voice was not hers. It belonged to someone else, and she no longer needed to experience it as her own. My client Janet expressed

---

5   Gary Renaud, *The Disappearance of the Universe* (Hay House, Carlsbad CA: 2002), p. 84.

her self-hatred by chronically overburdening herself. She made herself unimportant in the scheme of her life. To overcome her tendency toward being everyone else's doormat, Janet had to battle ferociously against internal voices that told her she wasn't doing enough or that she was a failure whenever she wasn't meeting at a level of two hundred percent what she perceived as others' demands.

A woman named Kerry came to see me after she had undergone surgery to remove a cyst on her right ovary. She had suffered pain on the right side of her pelvis for about a year. Doctors had identified the cyst, told her the pain was a result of the cyst, and removed it. Unfortunately, the pain continued. The doctors had identified a symptom of the problem, but not its cause.

When I palpated Kerry's body, I noticed that the connective tissue and muscles in her pelvis and abdomen were severely contracted. Connective tissue contraction can produce localized pain. It can also cause the growth of cysts and tumors, since compression in any area of the body inhibits blood and lymph circulation and the removal of toxins. Connective tissue tension can result from physical trauma, biological trauma, emotional trauma or some combination of these. Kerry's pelvic pain was due primarily to early emotional trauma unintentionally inflicted by her mother.

Kerry's mother had made a regular practice of giving her daughter enemas. As a child, Kerry had hated this. The more the mother gave the daughter enemas, the more the daughter reacted by subconsciously constricting her abdomen and pelvis in fear, anger and pain. This constriction eventually became habitual. Years later it resulted in chronic pain and possibly contributed to congestion that promoted the growth of a cyst.

Later in life, Kerry unconsciously repeated patterns of childhood abuse by inviting invasion into her pelvic area. As a child, she had let her mother give her enemas that she did not want, because she had no choice. As an adult, she let the doctors perform a surgery that her intuition told her at the time that she did not need. She had not listened to her intuition, perhaps because she had a habit learned in childhood of giving her own opinions no weight. Her intuition however had been accurate, and the cyst surgery did not resolve the pain from which she suffered.

Healing for Kerry required her to re-experience how awful the childhood enemas had been for her. As she dropped into this experience in a bodywork session, tears flooded her eyes and her pelvis softened. In this moment, Kerry had her first experience of being compassionate toward herself. Instead of judging or controlling how she felt, she just let herself live the emotional anguish she had for so long suppressed. She had spent years minimizing how she felt. In those years, as she blocked herself from feeling, her emotional distress had morphed first into tension, then into severe tension, and finally into crippling pain. As she now let herself feel the emotional pain, the physical pain eased.

Having stuffed her anger over the enemas for so many years, Kerry had turned that anger against herself. She was angry at herself for not speaking up for herself as a child when her mother wanted to give her enemas that she did not want. She was angry at herself for not speaking up for herself as an adult when the doctors convinced her to undergo an operation she felt she did not need. And she was angry at herself for not getting better sooner. She was just plain angry.

Kerry had a critical realization in her journey toward healing when she recognized that whenever she felt anger toward herself, her pelvis and torso tightened. She saw then that her anger toward herself was creating her pain, and that if she wanted to get well, she was going to have to give up her self-hatred. If she wished to let go of the pain of feeling controlled as a child, she also had to let go of the pain of controlling herself through self-criticism.

Anger toward yourself is cruel. It contracts you, putting you in a vice. Self-criticism is just another way to experience mutilation. The moment we first glimpse this fact is a moment of profound truth, and it presents the hardest challenge we must face in order to heal: the challenge to move from belittling ourselves to caring for ourselves.

Self-hatred and guilt damage you emotionally, mentally and viscerally. You abuse and victimize yourself when you indulge in these feelings. When you can be sufficiently present to your body so as to be able to observe the somatic impact of negative feelings, you begin to perceive how viciously you treat yourself when you have them. Only compassion and forgiveness—toward oneself as much as toward others—can heal the wounds of life.

Exercise: Let go of self-hatred

Remind yourself daily that all negative emotions toward yourself are forms of self-hatred. Most people's self-criticism runs so deep that they hardly recognize it. When you hear a negative self-critical voice in your head, try to distance yourself from it. Flowers don't judge themselves, even if their bloom isn't quite perfect, and neither should you. If you can contact the physical feeling in your body that goes along with your self-critical and self-punitive inner chatter, you will recognize that it is a contraction, and that all contraction acts as a vice on your life force.

Releasing Self-Punitive Patterns

Being a victim is part of the human drama. We are all like Emily, Janet and Kerry in one regard: as dependent children, we find some way to make ourselves responsible for the wounds we receive from life. This makes us self-punitive. It takes us a long time to recognize our own self-punitive behavior for what it is. Part of doing so is recognizing that it is normal, if only because it is inevitable, to experience trauma, especially as dependent and helpless infants or children. Therefore it is also normal and healthy to release and heal from trauma by identifying and letting go of our patterns of self-victimization.

Many years ago I had a personal healing crisis that revealed some of my deepest patterns of self-victimization and self-hatred. The origin of these patterns lay in my earliest experiences. Like

Janet, I had had a difficult birth. A twin, I was born six weeks premature, weighing three and a half pounds, and I was kept in an incubator for the first week of life. Because of various complications I was also in and out of the hospital a number of times in the first year of my life. These experiences created both a physical and an emotional tendency toward weakness and pain.

When I first began exploring craniosacral therapy as a healing modality for myself, several of my sessions on the therapist's table triggered memories of my birth and revealed the enormous influence that this dramatic experience had had on me. The emotional releases I experienced while reliving these memories, along with the immediate resolution of pain that resulted, played significant roles in my own decision to become a craniosacral therapist and to share the value of this therapy with the world.

In one of my craniosacral therapy sessions, I spontaneously entered an altered state that regressed me to the time of my birth, and I relived coming through the birth canal. My mother had told me that I had been a breech birth, and I knew that I had been born with scoliosis, but in my altered state I re-experienced both the trauma of the breech birth and the possible origin of my scoliosis. In my altered state, as I was moving through the birth canal, I felt a sudden, excruciating torque of my pelvis accompanied by severe pain in the right side of my lower back, as I relived the doctor pulling me out by the legs.

In my normal life as a child and young adult, I had no awareness of pain in my pelvis, and no memory of this experience. In my thirties, however, low back pain in my right side became a chronic pattern, and exercises and physical therapy did little to alleviate this pain. Spontaneous regressions to my birth provided the first systematic relief I had. After sessions that took me back to my birth or to the early days of life, I frequently experienced long periods of freedom from pain. Unfortunately, however, even though that freedom was significant, it was not lasting. I had to explore more deeply the impact of my earliest experiences to discover some missing links.

These links became clear over time as I carefully observed what was going on inside me when I had pain. First, I became aware that although the pain in my back sometimes occurred after strong physical stress, a more common underlying cause was emotional stress. I realized that I felt physical pain when I was emotionally vulnerable and was having difficulty standing up for myself. The physical pain would start as an overall sensation of raw tenderness throughout my legs and low back, and then would escalate to spasms. One night as I lay in bed experiencing the warning signs of raw tenderness, I had a sudden flashback to my first weeks of life. This was exactly how I had felt then! I had been *raw and tender,* neurologically and neuro-muscularly underdeveloped. I had also felt helpless and isolated. No doubt my parents and the doctors had done their best to help me, but my experience as an infant in those first days of life was one of sheer pain and vulnerability. The imprint of this very early experience had left its mark. I had learned to associate pain with helplessness and helplessness with pain. Both had also been my earliest default positions.

When I had been literally helpless as an infant, I had been in pain. When I felt emotionally helpless as an adult, I reverted to my earliest associations with helplessness, which were pain. When pain came on, it intensified my feelings of being vulnerable and helpless, since now I was not only emotionally but also physically fragile. My feelings of emotional fragility then became masked and suppressed under feelings of physical fragility. I buried my emotional pain under physical pain. If anything, I told myself that if I felt emotionally fragile at all, this was only because I was at that time physically fragile!

How all this expressed itself in adulthood was that when my boundaries were crossed, instead of recognizing this, I would retreat into pain while trying to ignore the emotional issue involved. Usually, my back pain would lift when I could admit to myself that my boundaries had been violated, stop acting out my vulnerability by collapsing in pain, and instead speak up for myself in ways that were empowering, even if scary.

We all learn most through our difficulties, and for years, pain was my teacher, a signal of further healing that needed to occur in my core. I have always felt that nothing, not even the worst of experiences, happens by accident. There is a divine force working through all our experiences. Today, I experience pain rarely, but I am grateful for the many experiences that led to growth and healing when I learned the lessons behind the pain.

One of my last experiences of learning from pain happened a number of years ago, when, after attending an exercise class I felt a strain in my back that gradually intensified over the next few days. I recognized that I was not dealing simply with a muscle strain that goes away in a few days. There had to be something deeper going on here. And so one afternoon I lay down, relaxed deeply, and entered into a more intimate relationship with myself. I knew that the pain was connected to early experiences of vulnerability that had not completely healed. I realized that a piece of my personality was still that weak, helpless child who was desperately in need of care. The traumatized baby was still living inside me, and she needed to be cared for. Who was going to help her, if not me? I began talking to that weak, lonely child, and comforting her, telling her I was there for her, that I would help her, and she needn't be afraid. The pain gradually became less.

Over the next week or so, I continued to talk to and comfort that inner child whenever I felt her painful vulnerability. Then I made a further discovery. There was another completely different persona inside me, one that was controlling and cruel. That persona had also played a major role in creating my back spasms. She wanted to drive me, to compel me to perform, to force me to do things that I might not be able to do, to make me stand up and be strong. That persona had also been there from infancy, pushing me to survive, to struggle against and overcome my learned helplessness. She had certainly served me well at times. But she was also a slave driver, a hostile and critical voice inside me. She would periodically put my whole body into spasms of internal self-hatred and vicious self-control. It was as though that persona was saying "Get up!" "Pull yourself together!" "Perform!"

I had two people inside me: the excessively vulnerable and weak persona, and the adamantine persona that knew how to push, that hated the vulnerable self and did its best to control and belittle it. I had to heal both. So far, I had done a good job with the vulnerable persona, but the slave driver still occupied a place in my core. She was the same persona who had years ago driven me to perform brilliantly in school and to succeed in a profession that turned out not to be my true calling. I was never "good enough" for her. She was my internalized rage. If I was not only to survive but also to achieve the peace I wanted, she had to change. I decided to talk to her, just as I had talked to my vulnerable weak persona. Instead of comforting her, however, I would have to negotiate with her. I began a series of imaginary conversations. I told my slave driver how much I appreciated her. After all, she had originally shown up in order to help me survive. I told her I was grateful for her help. I also told her that she could see that by now, despite her good intentions, she was hurting rather than helping me. Perhaps she could see that the whip wasn't needed anymore, and since I knew her intentions were good, she might think of putting it down.

I treated my inner slave driver with care, consideration and respect. Why? People listen to others who give them respect. What's more, my internal slave driver had all along, in her own way, meant to help me. And so, I dialogued with my angry, punitive persona for a number of days. The remaining tensions and spasms in my back disappeared. The vulnerable child inside, split into the helpless victim and the raging tyrant, healed through the voice of love, understanding, compassion and negotiation.

Exercise: Release self-victimization

<u>What type of pain (neck, back, headache etc.) or illness is "typical" for you?</u> Are you susceptible to colds, to headaches or neck pain, to back pain, or to stomach

problems? While we all have physiological and biological weaknesses, consider the possibility that your symptoms might be a form of self-victimization. When you get sick or uncomfortable, could this be because you need to stand up for yourself in some way, or own your power, but are afraid to? Most of us have difficulty owning the confidence that is our natural right. What would happen if every time you got sick or felt poorly, you took the opportunity to ask yourself how you might be acting out insecurities or punishing yourself rather than speaking out on your own behalf or treating yourself with respect? This might help you replace any lingering weakness or fear with new and self-empowering strength .

The Trilogy of Emotional, Physical and Mental Bodies

Deep healing addresses the physical, the mental and the emotional manifestations of the underlying challenge of our lives that is fear. Every day I see examples of how deeply interdependent our mental, emotional and physical states are. A gentleman came to work with me after he was diagnosed with an inguinal hernia. From a medical point of view, Barry's hernia was the result of a weakening of the abdominal wall on the lower left side of his body. From a broader perspective, Barry's situation offered a valuable opportunity for self-healing and growth.

Barry was in the midst of trying to launch a major business enterprise that required a lot of patience and substantial risk. He was doing his best to deal with his understandable fear of possible failure. As we began to work together, it became clear that he manifested some of his self-doubt physically. He had a tendency to pull into himself, sometimes looking down rather than straight ahead when he talked, and walking fairly stiffly. Although fit for his age, he also leaned into his left hip. His body language was the expression of years of dealing as a shy person with an aggressive world: he pulled himself away from his center and turned to the left. Although this pattern was noticeable only to the trained eye, it also told me the history of the development of Barry's hernia. Over the years, his tension patterns had contracted the abdominal wall on the left side, eventually forcing a rupture due to the loss of abdominal space and consequent buildup of pressure on the internal organs.

Barry wanted to avoid hernia surgery, and this required a journey into letting go of fear on three levels: visceral, mental and emotional. Viscerally, we worked on correcting his tense body language and rebalancing his body through a series of Yoga exercises that he practiced diligently. Mentally, he began to work on recognizing that whenever he felt anxious, his mind chatter would increase. He saw that this affected the way he interacted with people in conversation. He would go into his "head" as he talked, retreating into himself by looking down to the left and losing the natural vivacity he showed when he was relaxed. This behavior also tightened his left abdominal area, where the hernia had developed. To reduce mind chatter, establish better contact with others, and inhibit his tendency to pull into the left side, Barry therefore worked on maintaining eye contact with people and breathing deeply. Since he tended to tighten up when emotionally stressed, he also practiced walking expansively with freely swinging arms and legs, letting himself radiate out from his center rather than pull in. The more he did this, the more he exuded confidence.

Barry never did have a hernia operation. Although his hernia is still there, it no longer bothers him. He solved his physical problem both by working with his body through daily Yoga exercises to rebalance his torso, and by changing some of his old habits of being in the world. Barry addressed the way he lived in his body. Above all, he learned how to expand rather than contract.

Physical problems can be profoundly symbolic. I became nearsighted in the same year that my parents divorced. Over the years my eyeglass prescription steadily increased, until at the age of forty I decided to work on reversing the process. I worked for two years with a behavioral optometrist who specialized in retraining the eyes. His primary goal was to improve my acuity by helping me reduce deep levels of visual and visceral tension. As I performed the exercises he gave me, I would periodically have flashbacks to experiences from my childhood. I realized that my loss of vision was directly related to things I hadn't wanted to "see." The more I reduced my visual tension, the more I could "see," both literally and metaphorically. My physical vision improved as my repressed emotions surfaced. As I get older, my vision continues to improve. I attribute this directly to my somatic self-awareness practice.

I worked recently with a client who had been diagnosed with acid reflux because of a chronic scratchiness in his throat and occasional difficulty swallowing. His voice also occasionally became hoarse. This man's problem was not related to acid reflux. It was related to chronic throat tension that he had developed from childhood as a shy boy growing up in a noisy household with controlling parents. He had learned to shrink into himself in his upper torso, neck and shoulders, in an attempt to handle the stress of his early experiences. Later, while he became very successful professionally, he continued to carry this tension in his throat, and it became worse under stress. He resolved his throat and voice problems as he learned first, to recognize that his issue was stress-based rather than the result of a biological problem and second, to release the chronic unconscious habit of tension that kicked in whenever he spoke. As a result, he also emanated greater calm and confidence.

Owning Your Vision

According to Raja Yoga, one of the primary goals along the road to self-liberation is to free ourselves from *samskaras*, tendencies that we have developed in this lifetime or earlier lifetimes that cause us suffering. *Samskaras* are past experiences and habits that keep us from our full potential by inviting us to continue repeating patterns that have not served us. The repressed experiences of Emily, Janet, Kerry and Barry all left deposits of tendencies that then repeated themselves in the present. My chronic back problems of earlier years were connected to childhood experiences of vulnerability and self-hate that repeated themselves whenever life presented me with a challenge to my self-growth, until I learned to see them clearly for what they were. The tendencies that Raja Yoga calls *samskaras* are manifested physically through visceral tensions, emotionally through fear and anger, and mentally through self-criticism and self-judgment.

Healing is about unlearning the *samskaras* that we have developed through fear-based experiences. When we approach life from this perspective it becomes an ongoing journey of emotional, mental and physical detoxification that gradually clears the lens of our perception, freeing us to feel loving, loved, peaceful and safe no matter what our situation. When we fully release our *samskaras*, we no longer see the world as a fearful place, and no longer feel unsafe. We own peace.

We want to hold on to pain and fear because we think we have to. We think these are real. Yet each of us is on a journey that involves courage and that will ask us to let go of our fear and our pain, even at times when this can seem extremely difficult. Every moment of our lives offers us a choice to move toward greater tranquility and peace or toward greater distress and fear. The river of life moves continually, and each moment we have a new opportunity to move in one direction or the other. Life's most difficult challenges are often opportunities to ground ourselves more deeply in the higher option, to take our faith and place it where it needs to be, in being at peace with ourselves and with what is. Where you put your attention is where you will go.

In the end, to fully own your freedom is to own your inner power and serenity to such an extent that the experiences of the world do not bother you. This power is not to be compared to stoicism, understood as the ability to bear life's hardships without complaint. It is a more active power positively to transform the meaning of our experiences, and then through this to transform our relationship to the world.

Motivational trainer Anthony Robbins is well known for his work showing people the transformational power of their minds. In one of his seminars, he inspires participants to use visualization and self-affirmation to perform fire walks. They discover that they can do something that seems impossible: they can walk across yards of smoldering, burning coals without damage to their feet. I have participated in a number of those fire walks, and am always amazed that my feet don't get burned. The value of fire walks is symbolic: they tell you that you can do what you think you can't do, but only if you decide you can.

Your mind is the most powerful tool you will ever have at your disposal, and your mind is ultimately in service to your heart. If you have a big heart, you have courage, and if you have courage, you can both live in the world at ease and move daily toward creating your own world rather than reacting to a world imposed on you.

When I was beginning to read about the power of the mind, I was fascinated by the story of Jack Schwarz, author of *Voluntary Controls*. Jack attracted tremendous attention in the early years of mind-body study. His abilities were meticulously observed, recorded and validated by the Menninger Foundation. Jack could plunge nails straight through his arms and pull them out the other side, without any change in blood pressure or any increase in sympathetic nervous system activity. His wounds healed almost instantaneously. His extraordinary ability manifested the power of the mind not merely to block out an uncomfortable experience, but to transform it. His body was impervious to the trauma of the piercing nails, reacting to it as if it did not exist.

At its highest level, the power of the mind is one with the supremacy of the spirit over the body. How had Jack learned this truth? He was no doubt born gifted. Yet it is also probably relevant that as a teenager and young man, he lived in Nazi-occupied Holland. This fact no doubt contributed to his learning early the importance of conquering fear. He lived at a dangerous time and place where one's life was constantly at risk, and he learned through self-study and discipline to quell the anxiety this must have created by focusing on developing his ability to control his body with his mind, and to vanquish the pain that could be caused by any attack on his body.

Exercise: Use the power of your vision

Explore being how you want to be. Your ability to see, feel and trust in where you want to go and how you want to be is a critical ingredient in your growth into freedom and joy. Practice daily seeing and feeling yourself as you want to be, no matter what the circumstances and struggles. You are finding your pole star. Keep it always in sight.

For audio support in developing your power of vision, download the *"Empowering Your Intention"* MP3 available on my website, www.ingridbacci.com or utilize my complete *Effortless Practice* CD or MP3 series on self-healing.

The Practice of Daily Emotional Healing

On the journey toward self-realization, all that counts is now. In each moment you have an opportunity to practice emotional healing from your fear, pain and other negative emotions. While some of this work might require seeking assistance in releasing and resolving repressed experiences, much emotional healing involves a daily practice that you can pursue on your own. This daily practice, which yields optimal results when integrated with the other practices mentioned in this book, has four aspects.

The first aspect of emotional healing lies in the ability to observe your emotions with more detachment. This practice of emotional detachment is similar to learning greater mental detachment or what was described as non-attachment in Chapter 4. In the same way that you might observe your mind racing without reacting to your thoughts, so, too, you can observe your emotions while working to reduce your reactivity. Since your emotions lodge themselves in your body, you pay attention to your body in order to observe your emotions accurately. It was my own practice of emotional detachment, for example, that ultimately enabled me to identify and dialogue with, rather than react compulsively to, the two parts of myself that were the helpless infant in pain and the self-punitive angry part of myself.

To develop your ability to observe your emotions with greater detachment, when you feel anxious, angry, afraid, resentful or impatient, you notice what these feelings are in your body. Do they involve a tightening in the chest or abdomen? A tensing of the jaw? Stomach palpitations? Sweating? You observe the sensations without judgment. You are learning how to accept, and through acceptance to dissolve, your attachment to these feelings, along with the tendency to repeat them addictively.

People can get stuck in their emotions when they want to know why they have them or when they start trying to justify, explain or analyze them. This is mental rumination that keeps you from moving forward. What your negative emotions are, how they control you, how they hurt you, and how to release them all become clearer if you just pay attention to what they feel like in your body without trying to dissect them. Negative emotions are synonymous with visceral turbulence. Just as the mind releases its obsessive thoughts if you observe them with detachment, so too emotions become less powerful if you take the time to simply notice how they feel without reacting to them.

The practice of detachment lays the ground for the second aspect of healing from negative emotions. This involves becoming more conscious of the self-destructive quality of your negative emotions, and then using this awareness to help yourself release the emotions more effectively, rather than remaining addictively attached to them. For example, when you feel anger, do you notice tension in your jaw, chest or stomach, a tightening of your neck, or some other form of discomfort? Can you see that such feelings either involve self-punishment of some sort or a failure to take responsibility for how you feel? Can you see that even though you may feel justified in your anger, it actually contracts and tightens your body? Do you need to change what you do in response to situations in order to release the negative emotion? Or do you perhaps need to learn how to stay in some situation without letting it control you emotionally? Can you find a way to release the tension and then perhaps express how you feel or what you think with less of an unproductive emotional and mental charge? By paying attention to how your emotions feel in your body, noticing whether they involve unpleasant, contractive sensations, and working to release those in the many ways described in this book, you begin to heal your emotional addictions.

Even emotions we think are positive can involve subtle negative aspects. For example, when you notice feelings of excitement, do you feel tension? If so, that excitement is intimately related to fear. Can you feel the pleasure of excitement without feeling the tension that links excitement to fear?

The third practice of emotional healing involves directing yourself toward how you *want* to feel rather than toward how you *do* feel. You train your mind to align with where you want to go emotionally rather than with where you tend to go compulsively and habitually. Where we all want to go is toward peace, serenity, and joy. Developing the skill to go there is a matter of practice. The more you practice inner stillness through meditation, breath awareness and tools for body alignment described in Chapter 5, the stronger becomes your ability to replace negative feelings with more peaceful, life affirming ones, no matter what external obstacles tempt you toward anxiety, depression, disappointment or anger. In addition to training your body into greater states of internal tranquility through physiological relaxation, Yoga, the Alexander technique and more, you can strengthen inner stillness by remembering and visualizing states of peace, joy and centering that you have had in the past. By calling up past positive experiences into your imagination, you change your internal state. You learn how to shift from more negative to more positive states. If you do this systematically, eventually you will no longer feel the need to work on shifting internal states from negative to positive by recalling the sensations of past positive experiences. You will have learned how to direct yourself automatically and habitually toward internal power and peace rather than toward disempowerment and tension. At this point, the power of inner stillness and strength is great enough to make your negative emotions become increasingly insignificant. You have learned that underneath the turbulence is peace, and that only this peace is real. This is also your entry into love, since all true love is founded on inner contentment.

The fourth aspect of the practice of releasing negative emotions is learning to own peace in your communications with others, and to communicate without judgment. The practice of inner peace teaches you that all human beings are your brothers and sisters. Treating them as brothers and sisters does not mean, however, that you become a doormat, and valuing inner peace above all things does not mean that you become weak and passive in your daily life. Rather, when you have differences with others, you neither suppress these differences nor do you express them through attacking others or defending yourself. Instead, you are able to state your differences lovingly, yet also clearly, calmly and firmly. You cannot be supremely peaceful without being supremely strong, and you cannot be supremely strong without being supremely peaceful.

When conflicts appear in your life, they come as teachers. Their role is to help you learn that there is nothing to fear. Along the way, you may learn a piece of that lesson by standing up for yourself with a difficult colleague, family member or friend, and doing so tranquilly but firmly. You may also learn a piece of that lesson by beginning to see how your own defensiveness contributes to the difficulty you have with that colleague, family member or friend. Eventually, you find that the less you approach the world with fear or other negative emotions, the more responsive and kind the world is. The world does indeed reflect your inner state.

Exercise: Empower clear and calm communication

On your road to inner peace and strength, your biggest challenge lies in owning that peace in your communications with others. Who do you know who tends to raise negative feelings in you: feelings of anxiety or anger, irritation, etc.? Remember that no matter how that person behaves, your negative feelings are your own responsibility, and not theirs. Can you imagine talking to this person without anger, anxiety or frustration? Can you say what you need to say, and owning your space, without injecting negative feelings into what you say? Practice doing so in your imagination, until you find yourself able to do so in reality. By doing so, you will greatly improve both your own internal state and the effectiveness of your communications.

Summary

Emotional healing is at the core of all full spiritual growth. As you learn the techniques of mental calming and physical healing explored in earlier chapters, you inevitably also uncover the deposits of emotional wounds created by the traumas inevitably endured in the course of a lifetime. These emotional wounds, recorded both in the negative feelings that tend to plague each of us and in the corresponding constrictions and discomforts of our bodies, represent the final hurdles in our journey toward full authenticity and self-ownership.

You heal from your emotional wounds by recognizing and learning to release all forms of self-victimization, along with any corresponding tendency to victimize others. This chapter has explored some of the many forms that self-victimization can take, and the way this punitive relationship to ourselves registers itself in the body, including in the form of physical pain and illness. Your challenge, as you explore your own patterns of negativity and self-victimization, is to learn full self-acceptance, and to grow from that into the strength, peace and confidence, as well as physical vitality, that are your birthright. The clearer you are about your desire to release yourself from all forms of negativity, both toward yourself and toward others, and the more you practice tools that help you do this, the more swiftly you move along the path of your self-liberation.

CONCLUSION

Life is a journey. That journey has only one destination: yourself. You know you have found yourself, and can fully be yourself, when you live from a place of peace. When you find this place, you can be active and productive, and yet at peace. You can be at peace, and yet also be active and productive. You can be at peace even though the world around you is full of conflicts, and even though you must deal with these every day. You are equally peaceful in times of adversity and in times of prosperity.

What, after all, is it to be at peace? It is nothing more nor less than to be fully centered and at one with yourself, through all the storms and eddies of life. We are not meant to control either our own lives or the lives of others. We are meant to flow with life and to be a part of it. We are cells in the giant organism of the universe, and our task is to learn to play our part. When we play the part that we are uniquely and truly meant to play, we no longer feel resistance. We no longer suffer from tension, fear, anxiety, anger or despair. We have found and embraced our proper place in the universe.

Currently we live in a world founded on the opposite of peace. We live in a culture that fosters and thrives on fear. In the end, it is fear, and fear alone, that takes us away from ourselves. Fear causes us to seek to establish our worth through how we are seen by others, through material possessions, or through our accomplishments. The recognition of others, material well-being, and a life of productivity are all wonderful things to have. But they cannot act as a healthy and secure foundation for our sense of self. Our grounded sense of self can only result from our own pursuit of our inner freedom and full self-expression. Otherwise, recognition, financial well-being, and professional status become fetters to our souls, the chains that bind us and keep us from a genuine exploration of ourselves and from finding our unique foundation and purpose.

To discover yourself you must learn step by step to challenge fear in all its forms, and through this process to learn the peace that comes as the result of releasing yourself from turbulence. By learning to observe and release mental, physical and emotional turbulence, you come to a clearer understanding of the fact that you are already whole and complete. You begin to journey through life with the deep confidence that comes from knowing you are whole, and with the loving kindness toward others that is a natural result of this knowing. You find your place. You find yourself. You find home. And in finding home, you begin easily and naturally to find abundance in all spheres of life.

The preceding chapters have offered you a pathway toward yourself, the only place that can possibly offer you true shelter. May you travel safely on the road, and may your step every day grow stronger and more sure. Everyone here on earth needs your strength and clarity of purpose, as you need theirs. May we all meet the challenge of living fear-lessly in the universe that is our abode.

ABOUT THE AUTHOR

Ingrid Bacci is an internationally recognized author, somatic healer, and inspirational trainer of physical, emotional and spiritual self-actualization. Her two previous books, *The Art of Effortless Living* (Perigee, 2002) and *Effortless Pain Relief* (Simon & Schuster, 2005), both of which are translated into numerous languages, have been Book of the Month Club selections and have been featured in Oprah's magazine *O*. Ingrid offers retreats internationally on self-healing and self-actualization, and trains practitioners in the healing arts. She offers private sessions both in person and on the phone, to help clients identify and address core issues involved in their healing.

Ingrid's expertise grew out of deep personal experience. After graduating with highest honors from Harvard University and receiving a doctorate from Columbia University, Ingrid had started a career as a college professor when she became crippled by a severe connective tissue disease. When medical care failed to help her, she embarked on an exploration of bodywork, mind-body techniques and spiritual study that healed her completely. This process also initiated a radical career shift. Certified in the Alexander Technique and in Craniosacral therapy, Ingrid has integrated these complementary disciplines, along with deep knowledge of Yoga philosophy and practice, into a unique approach to integrative healing. Through her lectures, workshops, individual consultations and educational products, she seeks to help others use self-awareness to enhance personal empowerment, physical, mental and emotional health, and spiritual self-realization. Further information can be found on her website, www.ingridbacci.com.

Ingrid lives in Cortlandt Manor NY, and devotes her free time to hiking, nature preservation, and community building.